THE NEW GUIDE
TO SCREENPRINTING

THE NEW GUIDE TO SCREENPRINTING

BRAD FAINE

Foreword by Peter Blake CBE RA RDI

HEADLINE

A QUARTO BOOK

First published in Great Britain in 1989
by HEADLINE BOOK PUBLISHING PLC

HEADLINE BOOK PUBLISHING PLC
79 Great Titchfield Street
London W1P 7FN

British Library Cataloguing in Publication Data
The new guide to screenprinting
1. Screen prints. Techniques
764′.8

ISBN 0-7472-0156-0

This book was designed and produced by
Quarto Publishing plc
The Old Brewery
6 Blundell Street
London N7 9BH

Senior Editor Cathy Meeus
Editor Patricia Seligman

Designer Anne Fisher

Picture Researcher Arlene Bridgewater
Photographer Ian Howes

Art Director Moira Clinch
Editorial Director Carolyn King

Typeset by QV Typesetting
Manufactured in Hong Kong by Regent Publishing Services Ltd
Printed by Leefung-Asco Printers Ltd, Hong Kong

Foreword

Making a print is always the result of cooperation between artist and printer, and in my experience this is particularly true of screenprinting. I have only completed about 25 screenprints, one set of etchings (plus two or three odd ones) and one set of wood engravings. I also am currently making some wood engravings to illustrate a private press edition of *Under Milk Wood* by Dylan Thomas.

With wood-engravings you are on your own — no one else can help you cut the blocks. I taught myself to do it from books and by remembering the one or two lessons I'd had 30 years earlier as an art student. Although Cliff White of White Ink Studios printed the blocks beautifully, and Gordon helped with the graphics and folder, the main effort was mine.

I was taught to etch by Aldo Crommelynck in Paris, who is recognized as one of the best etchers in the world. Together we produced a set of nine etchings called *James Joyce in Paris.*

This couldn't have happened without Aldo's skill, and the finished prints were a joint effort.

By contrast, all the screenprints I have done have been made by a printer from an original work of mine — usually a watercolour — which I have then proofed. Although I have not literally printed my own prints, I have been extremely lucky to have worked with masters of screenprinting, and to have been involved with some of the most important events connected with the development of British screenprinting.

Chris Prater, who taught screenprinting at Hornsey School of Arts from 1958 until 1962, started a commercial studio in 1958, producing screenprinted show-cards, posters, etc. In 1961 Gordon House asked Chris if he would make screenprints for him: these must have been the first fine art screenprints of that period. Later both Eduardo Paolozzi and Richard Hamilton worked with Chris. Then in 1963 Richard Hamilton put together a portfolio of screenprints by 20 different artists for the Institute of Contemporary Arts (ICA) and I was invited to participate. I'm sure the ICA portfolio, printed by Chris Prater, changed the course of printmaking. Twenty artists made screenprints who might otherwise never have done so: some of them went on to produce a great many prints in the screenprint boom that followed. I worked with Chris Prater again when he printed my eight watercolour illustrations to *Alice Through the Looking-Glass.*

The other important event in modern screenprinting history that I was associated with was the Visual Aid print for Band Aid, which was printed by Brad Faine, the writer of this book, at his Coriander Studio in 1985. It is a beautiful and, I find, still moving, print that I am grateful and proud to have been involved with.

I treasure my association with the world of screenprinting, and with the magicians who did all the work in making prints from my paintings. This guide to screenprinting by Brad Faine is most informative, as well as being enjoyable. It has given me new perspectives into the diversity of creative possibilities of the medium and a fresh insight into the techniques used to produce some of the most effective printed images of recent years. I have learnt a great deal from it!

Maybe I should make some more screenprints — and perhaps I might even print them myself!

Peter Blake CBE RA RDI

Above *Self-Portrait with Badges,* 1961. Oil on board by Peter Blake.

Left *Well isn't this grand....*One of a series of eight screenprints made by Chris Prater from Peter Blake's watercolour illustrations to *Alice Through the Looking-Glass.*

Contents

Part One

INTRODUCTION TO SCREENPRINTING

Over the centuries screenprinting has developed from its crude
early form as a method for printing crusaders' banners to its more
recent incarnation as a system of producing sophisticated fine art works.

Origins of screenprinting

The development of screenprinting in the West can be traced from two separate sources; the oldest is concerned with stencil making, while the more recent involves ink and fabric technology. The earliest evidence of the use of stencils is to be found in the Pyrenees in the Magdellenian Caves (14,000 — 9,000 BC), where negative hand prints have been found which were made by blowing pigment through a reed or bone around the outstretched fingers. In the ancient world stencils had such diverse applications as the decoration of the Egyptian tombs, the design outlines of Greek mosaics and, in classical Rome, in the lettering painted on wooden boards, publicizing attractions at the Games — an early form of advertising.

During the period of the six dynasties in China (AD 221 — 618) stencils were extensively used in the mass production of images of Buddha.

The Middle Ages witnessed an early form of screenprinting when tar was painted on stretched plain cloth and allowed to dry, forming a negative stencil. Paint was then forced with a stiff brush through the area free from tar on to banners or uniforms. The images produced tended to be simple motifs such as the crusaders' red cross.

JAPANESE INNOVATIONS

It is, however, with the import of Japanese wooden frames to the West in the mid-nineteenth century that the second and perhaps more orthodox historical development begins. The ability to attach stencils to a fixed mesh meant that intricate designs could now be accurately registered and stipple painted with a brush. An early exponent of this technique was William Morris, who used it for screen printing on to fabric. In 1907 the first patent was granted to Samuel Simon for a system of stencil making using filler painted directly on to the screen. This technique permitted a more finely detailed stencil. Shortly after this the squeegee was invented, enabling a more consistent deposit of ink to be printed than had been

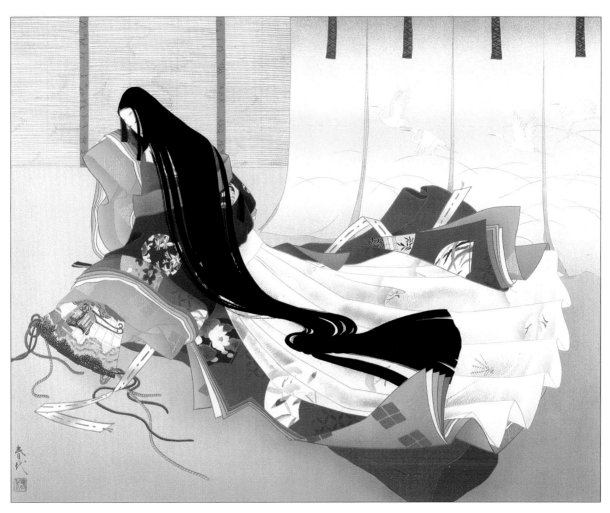

HARUYO
Twelve Layer Kimono

This traditional Japanese image was
realized using modern screenprinting
techniques.

possible with the stippling brush. During the First World War the medium was used extensively in the production of banners and pennants.

MACHINE - VERSUS HAND-MADE STENCILS

The first photostencils of 1915 paved the way for an expansion of screenprinting into the graphic design market. Using this method, "point of sale" material that was cheap and of high quality was produced for the chain stores of the 1920s. The connoisseur approach to printing, such as etching or lithography, collapsed with the stock market crash of 1929. The depression that followed meant that artists had to produce inexpensive items for home consumption so they turned to screenprinting, working on projects often financed by government bodies.

Hand-made prints of this period were usually made by painting directly on to the screen (gum and tusche method see page 39). To differentiate between hand-made images and those produced by commercial printers, the artists called them "serigraphs".

"OP" TO "POP"

In the 1950s Luitpold Domberger, an entrepreneur printer/publisher in Stuttgart, offered his studio services to artists such as Joseph Albers, Willi Baumeister and Victor Vasarely. Domberger took what had been a primitive medium and refined it to produce accurately printed, highly finished works of art, later referred to as "Op Art". At the same time in the United States, Jackson Pollock and Ben Shahn experimented with the medium but found that collectors and dealers were prejudiced against it. However, this attitude radically changed in the 1960s when Andy Warhol, Roy Lichtenstein and Robert Rauschenberg started using the medium to produce now familiar "pop" imagery.

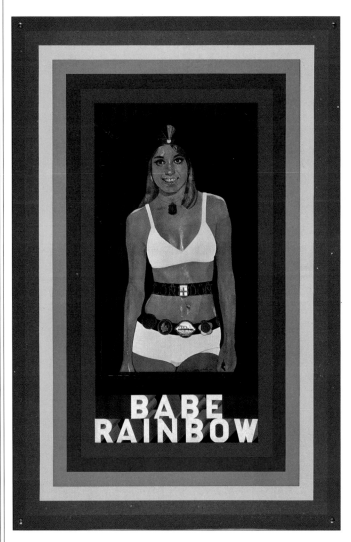

PETER BLAKE
Babe Rainbow

Peter Blake was a founder member of the
Pop Art movement in Britain known
for his combinations of popular imagery.

EDUARDO PAOLOZZI
Bash

Paolozzi's Bash, standing for Baroque All
Style High, is typical of his early
screenprints.

KELPRA STUDIO

A parallel development was taking place in Britain with artists such as Richard Hamilton, Eduardo Paolozzi, R B Kitaj and Joe Tilson working with Chris Prater at the Kelpra Studio. The Institute of Contemporary Arts encouraged this experimentation by financing a portfolio of 20 screenprints by leading artists of the period, including Richard Smith, Peter Blake, Peter Phillips as well as those already mentioned.

The 1970s heralded a technological revolution with the introduction of thin film inks and ultrafine meshes. These innovations permitted a precision in detail to be achieved as a matter of course (ie 133 half-tones). This decade also witnessed a rise in popular interest in limited edition prints and a resulting proliferation of small galleries selling such work.

The depressed economic climate of the early 1980s caused the demise of many of these galleries and halted the increase of print studios. During this period, artists and printers continued to experiment, extending the frontiers of the medium.

There is renewed hope for the screenprint artist in the late 1980s with a revival of interest in prints. This is due largely to the expansion of the market in the United States, the Far East, and the corporate market's interest in prints as an investment. This expansion has had two contradictory effects on screenprinting. First, edition sizes have increased and, secondly, some artists have returned to working directly on stencil making, producing small editions or even monoprints.

JOE TILSON
Sun Signatures

Enlightened by Chris Prater in 1962 to
the potential of the screenprint, Joe Tilson
went on to become one of its chief exponents.

R B KITAJ
Addled Art Minor Works Volume VI

Also working with Chris Prater at the
Kelpra Studio, Kitaj was a prolific
producer of screenprints in the 1960s.

What is a screenprint?

Screenprinting is one of the simplest forms of print-making available to the artist. It involves the use of a stencil applied to a fabric mesh stretched over a rigid rectangular frame. Ink poured into the frame is forced with a squeegee through the open areas of the stencil. This action produces an image when the underside of the screen comes in contact with the printing material (or stock).

THE STENCIL

In order to determine what an image will look like, it is important to understand that the areas that are missing from the stencil are what will appear on the print. A stencil at its most basic may be a sheet of thin paper (ideally newsprint) with, say, a hole torn in the centre of it, which is then taped to the underside of the screen. Because stencils are the means by which artists' ideas are translated into prints, it is important to understand how they work.

An easy introduction to stencil making is to be found in traditional letter form stencils. If the letter A is cut from a stencil it leaves a negative image that when printed becomes positive. Alternatively, if the surrounding area of the letter is cut away leaving a positive image, the resulting print will be negative.

The obvious drawback of stencils is that bridging pieces are necessary to prevent any "floating" pieces from falling out of the main body of the stencil — for example, the triangle in the top of the A. The problem of bridging pieces was initially solved by using human hairs to support the floating elements of the stencil. Later silk fabrics stretched over wooden frames replaced these hair grids. But it was from the frames brought to Europe from Japan in the mid-nineteenth century that the screen for printing through was developed.

BRUCE McLEAN
Pipe Dream 1984

This three-colour screenprint shows how even a simple image can have both dramatic and graphic impact.

Basic screenprinting
As an example of a basic screenprint, the letter F has been cut out of a piece of paper and fixed to the underside of the screen (1). Ink is pressed with a squeegee through the open part of the screen, that is, through the F shape (2). This prints a positive image of the letter on the sheet of paper placed beneath the screen (3).

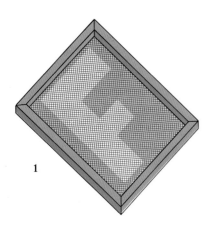

1

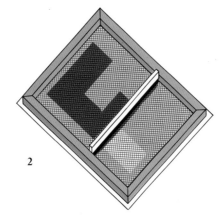

2

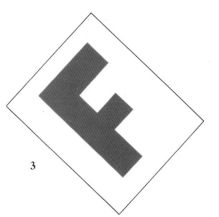

3

Print or reproduction?

The increase in edition sizes in recent years has led to a blurring of the difference between an original print and a reproduction. A reproduction is a facsimile of the image from which it is made — for instance, a copy of a painting printed in a book is a reproduction. Similarly a painting or drawing printed for a poster using the four-colour photographic process is a reproduction.

The criteria used by the United States Customs for determining whether a print is an original (on which no duty is paid) or a reproduction (which incurs duty) are quite specific: if the colours are individually separated and printed one after the other, it is an original. If the four-colour or half-tone process is used without any additional input by the artist, it is a reproduction. In Europe the criteria are slightly more relaxed in that a print is deemed to be original if the artist intended that any preliminary work was made exclusively for subsequent printing such as Ilana Richardson's watercolour (see page 115). Under this definition photographic processes may be used in the production of the image.

FINE ART PRINT

The fine art print can either be a work which is developed or translated from another source (a point of departure such as an artist's drawing or watercolour) or it may be created through the medium itself, in which case the artist will make a number of stencils and progressively proof them until a satisfactory print is made. In the latter case the "original" is the finished print. Prints may be developed from concepts, photographs, drawings, experimentation on the screen itself, or simply randomly juxtaposing images. Whatever the source, printing will generate accidental discoveries often to the benefit of the print.

ILANA RICHARDSON
Raffles Garden 1988

This fine art print was developed from a watercolour painted by the artist. The original painting can be viewed as the point of departure and indeed the result reflects the medium used. But the range of techniques provided by the screenprinting process has allowed the artist, in collaboration with the printer, to go beyond the original concept.

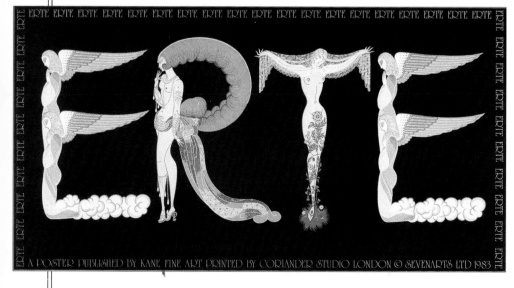

ERTÉ

An unlimited handmade poster using letter forms from the Erté alphabet.

Why make prints?

It is a good idea for artists to ask themselves why they want to make prints. For some it is the desire to work in a new medium, others want to acquire new skills, most recognize the potential of having their work seen by a wider audience across a broader geographical spectrum. But the important point to recognize when making an edition of prints is that they are made to be sold. Few people want to reproduce an image 60, 100 or 1,000 times out of creative interest. On the other hand it is important to realize that screenprinting is not merely a convenient reproduction process that can multiply an image prepared in some other way. For the artist-printmaker working directly with the medium it is a creative process in its own right; the challenge is to produce an image derived from the unique characteristics of that process.

The making of stencils means that the artist has to translate ideas rather than expressing them directly. If an artist paints a picture the colour is applied straight onto the canvas, whereas if a similar image is printed individual stencils have to be made for each colour. Far from inhibiting creativity, the practicalities of this process can provide an exciting stimulus. Technical limitations can be beneficial in that they may be turned to aesthetic advantage and exploited to develop personal vision. The scope for subject matter is infinite, if an idea or image can be turned into a stencil it may be printed. With practice an artist can develop this conceptual process into a new way of seeing.

Creative excitement is enjoyed alike by the professional artist working with technical help and sophisticated equipment and the novice screenprinter using home-made equipment on the kitchen table. Both will gain from the stimulus of making pictorial statements in a new or different way.

Working with stencils does not imply that prints must always be carefully contrived, but rather that the type of image will determine the degree of technical expertise. In some cases, it may be advisable to adopt a systematic approach and to analyse the print in an abstract or formal way. An alternative approach is to rely on intuition and simply print stencils as they are made, making judgements about them as each successive pull is taken. Learning to plan ahead to ensure that maximum effect is obtained from the minimum number of stencils may promote an intensity of creative effort that can lead to economically elegant results.

There are four options available when deciding on the size or type of editions to be printed. The **monoprint,** as its name suggests, is a unique work or art — a one-off. It may be created on the print bed as the print is being made or predetermined by juxtaposing a number of stencils. The critical factor is that it differs in its form as well as colour from any other print. If a print is made using the same stencils printed in different colours this is known as a **suite.** Suites can have any number of variations, but are usually limited by exhibiting space. A variation of the suite is the **multiple,** the refinement being that each print interacts with others to produce a larger work. Finally there is the **limited edition** where all the prints are similar to one another (see page 16). An edition is unlimited when an artist continues to produce signed prints as long as people wish to purchase them. Hockney's well-known *Parade* poster is an example of this.

DAVID HOCKNEY
Parade

This unlimited edition print was produced from hand-separated stencils from an original painting by the artist.

BRUCE McLEAN
Lobster Factor 10 Days 1-14

This hand-made autographic screenprint
is a limited edition that was developed
from a monoprint. It was created by the
artist working closely with the printer in a
professional studio. In such a partnership
the artist produces an idea which the
printer then translates into a printed image.

Limited editions

A limited edition is a run of prints limited to a certain number with each print individually signed by the artist. The prints are signed in pencil on the border, showing that the print is of acceptable quality to the artist, and numbered in a way that proves the authenticity of the edition size — 15/125 shows that a particular print is number 15 of an edition of 125.

In the past an edition was by convention less than 100 copies. This originated from the days of purchase tax; when 99 prints were classed as "art objects", which were not liable for tax, and a 100 or more as "fancy goods", which were. The size of an edition these days can be 10, 100, 10,000 or as many as the artist cares to sign. However, there are other factors that affect edition size.

CREATING VALUE

Originally prints were limited to small editions by the technology of their production. An etching plate would deteriorate after use and consequently early or low number prints were of superior quality to later ones. Modern print technology has enabled thousands of impressions to be taken from a print without any serious deterioration in its quality. Consequently, the number of prints in an edition has no effect on the intrinsic value of that item. So, the main reason for limiting an edition is to create a value for it.

Critics of limited edition prints claim that such artificial scarcity leads to an inflated value. But since the nineteenth century, it has been common practice to create value by signing and limiting editions. The artist is always free to break with the convention of signing and numbering prints. In this he has a suitably unconventional precedent in the person of Maurice Escher, who produced prints from an edition as and when people wished to buy them, sometimes he signed them, sometimes he refused. Whistler, an early exponent of this practice, produced both signed and unsigned copies of the same print. Those with the signature were sold for twice the price of those without.

Printing can make images freely available, economically speaking, but the danger then is that popularity could become the only criterion for production. The limited edition because of its potential high value allows the work of more esoteric artists to reach their minority audience.

Collectors and dealers collaborate in artificially enhancing rarity value. As the market for contemporary art is finite and fairly small, the prints of a successful artist are often acquired for investment as "a hedge against inflation". A collector con-

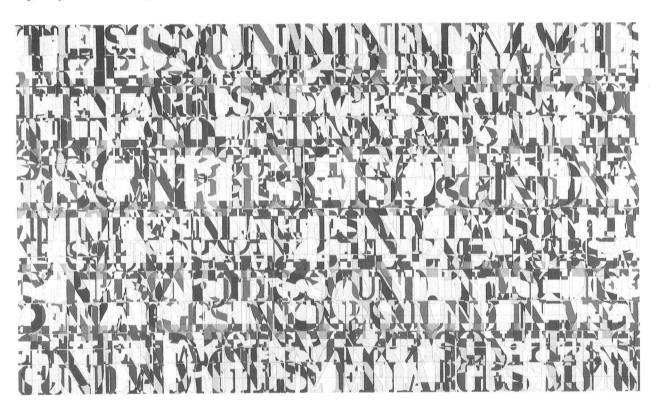

TOM PHILLIPS
The Sounds in my Mind

The stencils for this limited edition
screenprint were hand-made by the artist.
The artist and maybe the publisher would
decide on the size of the edition. Here the
edition was limited to sixty which is a
medium-sized run.

ERTE
L'Orientale

Probably one of the most profilic and
best-selling artists of screenprints, Erté
made this print in an edition of 300 with
50 proofs.

BRENDAN NEILAND
Lloyd's

This abstract view of the Lloyd's building
in London was developed from a painting
commissioned by Lloyd's.

cerned with investment will want to purchase an image which
is not widely available, in the hope that it will maintain its
value.

ECONOMICS OF PRINTING

The appeal to exclusivity, however, is not the only reason for
limiting an edition, another equally valid point concerns the
potential market size and the economics of print production.
The unit cost of a print falls dramatically as the edition size
increases as the preliminary origination and proofing costs
are the same for an edition of ten or 100 copies. So a publisher
usually tries to print the maximum number of impressions he
is able to sell. No publisher would wish to overestimate and
thereby accumulate prints for which there is no market. But if
an edition is small, the cost of production per print will be
correspondingly high.

The retail price of a print is a function of the costs of the
artist, printer and dealer plus a notional value relating to its
investment or decorative worth (see also Selling Prints, page
134). The majority of prints are purchased for decoration,
whether by individuals or corporate bodies, so that a

publisher is unlikely to reduce the size of the potential market
merely to inflate unit value.

THE PRINT AS AN INVESTMENT

The wider use of limited editions by large companies to com-
memorate events and sponsor artistic projects has led to an
expansion of interest in prints by the corporate market. But
contemporary prints are being recognized as a good investment in a wider context — for example, a 1967 Jasper John
print was sold in 1988 for $150,000. Fortunately, this invest-
ment potential has some worthy beneficiaries. For example,
the financing of the late Norman Stevens' print for the botan-
ical cultural gardens at Kew in London by Pirelli has helped
replace some of the trees uprooted in the storm of 1987. The
Visual Aid for Band Aid print is another example. For this
print 100 separate images, each donated by the artist, were
reduced in size and printed to form a single image. This was
then reproduced in an edition of 500 with all the proceeds
going to the Band Aid Trust. It was the first time that 100 artists' signatures appeared on the same print.

Other applications for screenprinting

Fine art editions are not necessarily two-dimensional, or printed exclusively on paper. A large number of artists make three-dimensional prints, projecting images directly on to sculpture or paintings. For example, from 1962 Andy Warhol made numerous screenprints directly on to stretched canvas for such works as the *Marilyn Diptych* or *Green Coca-Cola Bottles*. The extension of printing into three dimensions and perhaps combined with other materials inspires many artists.

COMMERCIAL USES OF SCREENPRINTING

In the commercial world screenprinting is found to be very versatile and is used on a wide range of surfaces from textiles, metal, wood, glass, Perspex or plastics to cardboard, bricks, plaster, rubber and canvas — in fact almost any surface. The screenprinting process is used in the ceramics industry for making transfers for the firing and direct screening of slips for pottery or ceramic decoration. The instant lettering used in design studios and dry release transfers played with by children are only available because of screen ink technology. But it is in the graphics industry that it is most widely employed — on vast hoardings, various aspects of advertising, information on equipment, and all sorts of decals and labels.

Printed circuits, essential to computers and household consumer durables, are screenprinted, taking advantage of the accuracy and precision possible with stainless steel meshes.

Screenprinting does not only work on smooth surfaces, walls, for example, can be decorated with images printed directly on them. Bottles and tins are printed directly on cylinder presses, plastics are often vacuum-formed after being printed with flexible ink, and decorated balloons are inflated with expanding ink images on them.

The use of the screenprint is fundamental to the textile industry whether for producing exclusive hand-printed fabrics or chain store materials, tee-shirts or designer logos.

Screenprinted textiles
The textile industry uses the screen-printing process for much of its pattern printing, not only for such exclusive fabrics as this chintz from the Laura Ashley range (above), but also for mass-produced items like tee-shirts (left).

Some of the more bizarre uses of the medium are to be found in the food industry, where cakes and sweets are sometimes decorated by printing with egg tempera and edible dyes.

NEW DEVELOPMENTS

New developments include touch-sensitive electronic inks, rub-off inks for competitions, and scratch and sniff inks for magazine advertisements or sensory films.

But it is the arrival of ultraviolet cured inks which has done most to open up new areas of activity. These inks remain wet until exposed to ultraviolet light, when they dry exceedingly quickly. This development has meant that high-quality book production and print runs, which were formerly appropriate only for lithographic printing, are being silk-screened, combining colour quality with a comparable printing speed to that of an automatic litho press. The future of screenprinting is only as limited as the vision of those who use it, and there will always be those who find new uses for it. Unlike the other established fine print mediums, such as etching, engraving and lithography, screenprinting is still in the process of building a tradition.

LIMITATIONS OF SCREENPRINTING

The development of thin inks and fine meshes means that there are very few images which are not possible to print. Indented or embossed lines cannot be printed by screening as the process requires pressure which is only obtained by direct printing, such as etching or engraving. Raised lines on the surface, however, can be produced using the appropriate ink and, as can be seen in Chapter 6, shapes can be embossed after printing.

The wash effect, produced by collotypes and to a lesser degree lithography, is difficult to produce in a single printing. But it can be approximated by sequential prints — the greater the number, the better the result.

The printing of continuous tone, irrespective of medium, requires for it to be broken down into small particles and printed as fine dots, either regular (in the case of half-tone) or irregular (for a mezzotint). Screenprinting can print a fine dot pattern (133 is possible), but lithography, etching and gravure can produce finer images.

Within these limitations almost anything can be printed. The difficulty is in determining how to make the stencil and deciding what sort of mesh should be used.

Part Two

PLANNING YOUR SCREENPRINT

The basic equipment required for screenprinting is minimal and need not be expensive. What is required is a frame stretched with fabric, a squeegee, some ink and something to print on — stock, such as paper. Having assembled the equipment, you will, of course, also need to plan the image you wish to print.

The frame

The frame is the support over which fabric is stretched; together they make up the screen. At its simplest, a frame can be made from a thick card rectangle with a smaller rectangle removed from the centre, covered on one side with a coarse organdie fabric that has been stuck to the card. This would be perfectly adequate for printing Christmas cards, or small images up to 15×20cm.

WOODEN FRAMES

The most readily available type of frame and the one chosen by most beginners is a wooden one, either home-made or custom manufactured. Making the frame yourself is not difficult but requires some basic joinery skills. An advantage of the home-made frame is that you can choose the size you require — 60×40cm is a good size to start with. The wood should have straight grain and not be warped — cedar is used by the commercial manufacturer as it is water resistant, rigid and light to handle. Make sure the weight of the wood is appropriate for the size of screen being made, as the fabric when stretched exerts a considerable tension. But the frame should not be too heavy to handle easily. The corners take the strain of the tension and should be properly glued and jointed (not

simply screwed or nailed). Finally, all wooden frames should be coated with a protecting finish that is ink and water repellent, such as polyurethane varnish or shellac mixed with methylated spirit (French polish).

READY-MADE FRAMES

If the cost of the artist's time is taken into account, it is probably more economic to buy a ready-made frame, unless you possess an adequate tool-kit and enjoy making things. The advantage of the manufactured frame over those made at home are that it will be made of the correct material, with the right ratio of cross section to frame, and with properly jointed corners (see below left).

Wooden frames can be purchased in 6in (15cm) incremental sizes from 62×8in (157×20cm) to 108×76in (274×193cm) as standard, and any other size by negotiation. The frame should always be the largest size that is practical since many small images can be put in a large screen, whereas obviously a large stencil will not fit into a small one. A wooden frame is easiest to work with for the printer who wishes to stretch his own meshes, as it can be tacked or glued depending on which stretching method is used (see page 24).

METAL FRAMES

Most professional printers use metal frames; they are more durable and, if correctly stretched, they make it easier to register prints correctly as they do not warp or bow under fabric tension. Wooden frames, even if they are professionally manufactured, will eventually flex and warp, causing stencils to distort.

Metal frames are made either of aluminium, which is light to handle but subject to distortion if clumsily attached to the printing table, or steel, which, if coated with baked on preserver, is the strongest and most durable material available. There are two main cross-section profiles: the box, which is rectangular, and the seriframe (see below). If a home-made print table is being used for printing (see page 59), a box section frame is best because it is more easily attached. If a professional printing table is used, the seriframe is stronger, more resistant to fabric tension and, because of its inside profile, easier to clean.

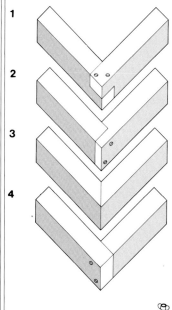

1
2
3
4

Wooden frames (left)
Wooden frames can be home-made or purchased from suppliers of printing equipment. The corners take the strain and therefore need to be glued and jointed properly. Illustrated here are four strong joints: (1) end-lap joint; (2) rabbet joint; (3) mitre joint; and (4) butt joint.

Master frame (below)
A master frame into which different frames can be fitted makes it easier to remove the printing frame for cleaning.

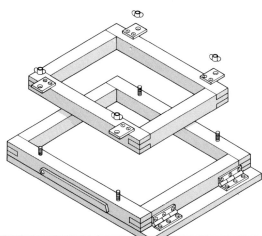

Metal frames
Metal frames are durable and are unlikely to bow under fabric tension. There are two cross-section profiles (1) the box frame and (2) the seriframe.

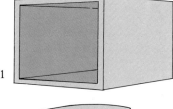

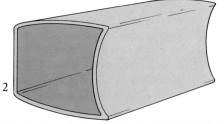

1

2

Meshes and fabrics

A wide range of materials can be stretched over the frame to make the screen. What you choose depends on the job you want it to do and on how much you want to spend. Organdie, silk, nylon, mono- and multifilament polyester or metal are all commonly used. The size of the mesh of the fabric is measured in threads per centimetre. The "mesh opening" is the distance between threads, and the "open area" the percentage of mesh openings to threads in an area of fabric.

FABRIC WEIGHT

The fabric you choose should be as strong as possible to avoid splitting when stretched, dimensionally stable and unaffected by moisture or humidity. The material should be inert and impervious to the chemicals to be used in contact with it. The greater the tensile strength of the fabric, the more consistently it will register, since it will resist distorting when the squeegee is pulled across it.

The weight of fabric is described by the letters T or HD (replacing the earlier system of lettering where S = fine, M = medium, T = heavy and HD = extra heavy duty). T now refers to standard duty, the most useful for fine art and hand printing, while HD or heavy duty is designed predominantly for long machine runs. An HD mesh with the same thread count as a T mesh requires greater squeegee pressure during printing and deposits a thinner film of ink due to the smaller mesh openings.

MESH COUNTS AND INK DEPOSITS

The mesh count limits the open area of the mesh, which in turn determines the quality of the ink deposit. A fine mesh with a high count, say 150T, allows only a thin film of ink to be printed, whereas a coarse one, say 42T, allows a heavy film. When planning your screenprint it is important to decide how heavily inked you want the print to be and what mesh count is appropriate for the job. Most professional studios use a range of about six different counts from 42T to 180T, but they may need to use a mesh as coarse as 20T to print glitter inks. The college or artist printmaker who is beginning to print editions will find counts of 62T and 90T are enough: the 62T for general areas and the 90T for fine work.

It is sensible practice to write indelibly on any new frame what the mesh count of the fabric is. If this is forgotten the count can be checked by using a mesh microscope or a linen proven to help to count the threads.

BUYING FABRICS

All fabrics are available in the roll from specialist suppliers (see page 140), in incremental widths from 1 to 2 metres wide. The minimum quantity normally sold is half a metre. The finest, most readily available fabric at present is 200T (200 threads per centimetre in a standard weight). Although this fabric is designed for use with ultraviolet inks, it can be used for a dot matrix of fine half-tones with suitably thinned conventional inks. Fabrics are usually available in white or antihalation orange or yellow for use with direct photostencils (see Chapter 3). This coloration prevents light from scat-

tering through the threads when the stencil is exposed to the ultraviolet source.

TYPES OF FABRIC

There are six different types of fabric suitable for making screens, each varying in character, cost and, in some cases, suitability for different uses.

Organdie is a cotton fabric, generally with a mesh count of 70 − 90 threads per inch. Because it is the least expensive option and is easy to stretch, it is ideal for the beginner.

Organdie can be obtained from haberdashers. It is suitable for use with cardboard frames to produce small prints such as Christmas cards. The limitations of this combination will quickly become apparent to the artist: the low tensile strength of the fabric and the fact that it expands when wet and contracts when dry, makes it difficult to register. Another disadvantage of organdie is that it deteriorates rapidly because it is attacked by most of the chemicals used in screenprinting.

Silk was the original fabric used for screenprinting; it is stronger than organdie. Silk should be moistened when stretching to obtain a really taut screen. In most situations silk is inferior to synthetic materials, except for the gum and-tusche method of stencilling (see page 39). Silk should never be used with photostencils as the bleach used in the process attacks the mesh.

Monofilament nylon fabrics are produced with finer threads or filaments than silk and are stronger and more elastic than those mentioned above. The elasticity is an advantage when printing on irregular surfaces, such as cer-

KATHERINE DOYLE
Quiet Evening

This screenprint was created using two different sizes of mesh: the variegated wash effect of the evening sky required a coarse mesh; the hand-painted areas were reproduced on a fine-meshed stencil.

amics, canvas or even bricks, but a disadvantage for tight "edge to edge" or butt register printing (see page 66). If properly stretched, nylon is a good general purpose material. It should not really be stretched by hand, as it requires a two-stage process: first it needs to be tensioned to the correct stretch and then allowed to slacken for 15 minutes. Then the centre needs to be dampened before finally completing the stretch and sticking the fabric to the frame.

Monofilament polyester is the best material to use for printing limited editions, because of the need for accurate registration. It is the strongest, the most dimensionally stable and chemically inert of all the non-metallic meshes. Like nylon it requires two-stage machine stretching to a higher tension than most fabrics and will accept all stencil materials if properly prepared. Multifilament polyester is used extensively in the textile industry and in the printing of large posters for hoardings when direct photostencils are used.

Stainless steel and nickel-plated polyester are the most dimensionally stable fabrics producing consistently accurate registration. They are mainly used for printed-circuit or similar precision work. However, they have disadvantages for the fine art printer in that they are expensive and crease if badly handled, making them useless for any stencil application. The rigidity of these materials prevents deliberate local distortion with tape to correct registration irregularities (see page 64). Metal meshes should be stretched professionally as they are expensive and it is better that the risk of splitting while tensioning is borne by the stretcher.

PETER BLAKE
Tattooed Lady

Artists will often combine a variety of mesh sizes within a single print. Here Peter Blake reproduces the dense areas of black and blue with a coarse mesh and the intricate detail of the tattoos with a much finer mesh.

Stretching the frame

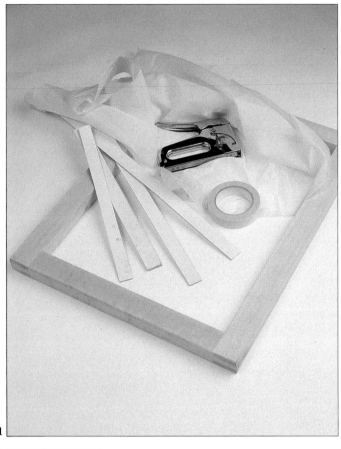

T he next step after obtaining the frame and selecting the fabric is to fix the fabric to the frame to make the screen, a procedure known as stretching the frame. For a wooden frame, the fabric can be stretched by hand, but a more professional result is obtained by using a mechanical roll-bar stretcher — an expensive piece of equipment. Metal frames have to be stretched using such a mechanical device. All frames can be stretched by a professional stretcher.

PROFESSIONAL STRETCHING

It may be preferable to have screens professionally stretched (see list of suppliers on page 140) as the advantages of doing this may outweigh the increased cost. If the screen is stretched professionally, you can rely on the fabric being correctly tensioned, properly adhered to the frame, and also correctly positioned with the threads running parallel to the edges of the frame, maintaining a right-angled grid pattern. The importance of this latter consideration becomes apparent when fine detail or dot matrix stencils are applied to an irregularly stretched fabric; the resulting print will have localized moiré patterns on it. Another advantage of employing a professional stretcher is that the customer pays only for the area of fabric used since screens are usually stretched in large numbers with little wastage. In the event of the fabric splitting due to excessive stretching, the replacement cost is borne by the company, not the customer.

1

2

3

4

5

Stretching a frame by hand
First gather together the tools and materials you will need: the frame, mesh fabric cut to size, staple gun, strips of card and masking tape or double-sided tape (1). Place the fabric on a clean flat table with the frame on top, checking that the weave is parallel to the sides of the frame. Stick the strips of card with tape along the edges of the fabric to prevent the staples from tearing it under tension. Now cut the corners of the fabric (2). Beginning with one of the long sides, fold the card over so that it is sandwiched between the fabric (3). Starting from the centre, staple along the frame ensuring that the fabric is stretched from the centre staple (4). Pull across and staple the opposite side and then complete the other two shorter sides (5). Finally, fold and staple like a canvas.

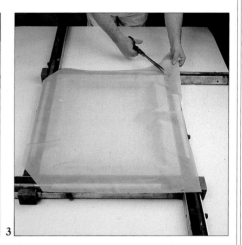

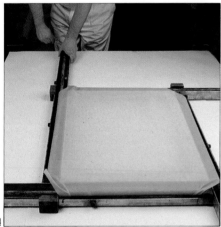

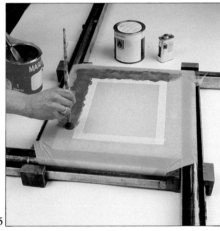

Stretching a wooden frame with a roll-bar stretcher
First the frame is placed on wooden spacers to adjust the height in the stretcher and the roll-bars adjusted to accommodate it (1). The mesh is fixed to the roll-bars with double-sided or masking tape (2). Next the corners of the mesh are cut (3). The roll-bars are turned in pairs until the correct tension is achieved (4).

Glue is worked through the fabric with a brush, sticking the fabric to the frame (5). Once it dries the mesh can be cut away so that the frame can be lifted out of the stretcher (6).

Professional stretching
Professional screen stretchers can handle large screens that would be difficult to stretch in a small studio. Here the tension of the fabric is being measured with a tension meter.

Preparing the mesh

Before using a newly stretched mesh, it should be properly prepared or the stencils will either fail to stick to it, or they will stick only partially. The fine detail on photostencils or twin-skin cut films tends to remain on the backing sheet when it is removed after drying if a screen has been inadequately processed.

Organdie and silk should be prepared when used for the first time by scrubbing the mesh with a soft brush and a proprietary household scouring powder, thoroughly rinsing off all the residue with cold water. Subsequent degreasing can be effected by washing the mesh with a 3 per cent acetic acid solution (vinegar). New nylon, polyester and steel should be prepared as described right.

RECLAIMING A SCREEN

To reclaim a screen, first all the old ink should be removed with the appropriate solvent. Next the tape and varnish must be removed. If the tape is of the cellulose type or an unvarnished gum-strip, this should be removed before proceeding to wash off any stencil material. The stencil, depending on its type, will be removed using solvent for spirit-based materials or water for soluble ones. Direct photostencil materials require specialized stencil removing agents. Indirect stencils may be removed with bleach diluted with water in the ratio of 1 part neat bleach to 3 parts water. Once the stencil has been attacked by the relevant chemical it should be removed with a jet of water, preferably under high pressure. Washing should continue until all traces of the stencil and ink have been removed. With some oxidization inks a residual image may have to be removed with "Haze Remover".

DEGREASING

Every time the screen is reclaimed it must be degreased on both sides. This is done by washing the mesh with either a degreasing agent or with acetic acid, which is left on the screen for a couple of minutes before being finally rinsed and dried. Household cleaners, methylated spirit and even alcohol can all be used for this purpose. The specialist prodducts for degreasing are the most efficient, but also the most expensive. Liquid agents are used rather than powder ones, which may leave a gritty deposit in the mesh and cause pinholes to appear in any stencil applied to it. The drying time can be reduced by blotting off the excess water with newsprint and air drying with a warm fan. Care should be taken to avoid touching the newly degreased mesh as even the cleanest hands have some oil on them.

TAPING THE SCREEN

To prevent ink from seeping between the edge of the frame and the mesh, it is necessary to seal this surface with tape. There are two ways of doing this. Cellulose parcel tape is quickest to apply and simplest to remove after printing. It is unaffected by ink, water or solvent. The more common and time-consuming way, however, is to use water-based gum strip which has the advantage of tightening the screen as it dries. This technique is described on the facing page.

Preparing nylon, polyester and steel meshes
These need to be abraded to ensure that the stencil sticks to the mesh. Proprietary "mesh preparation" powders or organic chemical pastes are produced by the ink manufacturers. (1) These preparations are toxic and harmful to the skin so wear rubber gloves, goggles and a breathing mask. Apply the powder or paste to both sides of the wet mesh. (2) Now scrub in the preparation with a nylon brush, before leaving it for a few minutes to react. (3) Next, rinse all trace of the preparation from the mesh.

Taping the screen

Water-based gum strip is cheap and it also tightens the mesh as it dries. (1) Wet the gum using a sponge strip and apply it first to the underside of the screen, covering the wood and about 2.5cm of the mesh. (2) For the top side, fold the tape in so that it covers both the inside edge of the frame and some of the mesh. (3) Make sure that the tape adheres closely to the corners and angles of the frame. (4) Water-based gum strip needs to be sealed with shellac. Extend the shellac 5mm over the mesh so that the ink does not seep under the gum strip.

The squeegee

The squeegee is used to press the ink through the open areas of the mesh and on to the paper below. The most basic form of squeegee is a straight, sharply cut piece of card. This is quite usable with the simple card frame for a beginner to experiment with. In the studio there are three types of squeegee in common use which come in various sizes to suit the purpose: the hand squeegee, the one-arm and the composite.

The hand squeegee is made up from a flexible blade inserted into a groove let into a wooden handle whose profile should be comfortable when being used. The squeegee is used to cut the surface of the ink cleanly, using the minimum pressure to produce a good-quality image. It should not be used to force ink through the screen under excessive pressure.

The one-arm squeegee is attached to the back of the printing table, and runs along a rail parallel to the front of it. This type of squeegee has the advantages of being easier to control than is the hand squeegee, less tiring to use when editioning, and it does not fall into the ink. Its disadvantages are that it makes blending more difficult (see page 70) and it is less sensitive to localized pressure if small areas of the stencil are proving difficult to print. Hand squeegees should not be used with one-arm units, as the extra pressure will often distort them.

The composite squeegee can be used for either hand or one-arm unit printing as the blade is held in metal grippers along its entire length. The composite squeegee can be taken apart for cleaning, but it is still easier to pre-tape the blade, rather than take the tool to pieces. An advantage of the composite squeegee is that it can have a number of small blades attached to it, and thereby enable you to print different colours on the same print stroke.

Hand squeegee (**top**) is a wooden handle fitted with a flexible blade, which is inserted into a groove let into the handle.

Composite squeegee (**above**) This type of squeegee has metal grippers to hold the blade and can be fitted with a number of small blades so that several colours can be printed with the same print stroke. This squeegee can be used for both hand and one-arm printing.

One-arm squeegee (**left**) Attached to the back of a printing table, a one-arm squeegee runs along a rail parallel to the front of it. This squeegee takes much of the strain out of printing large editions.

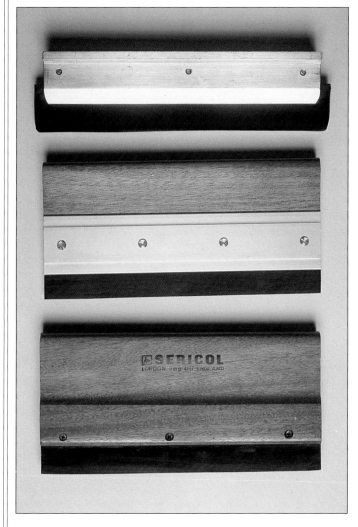

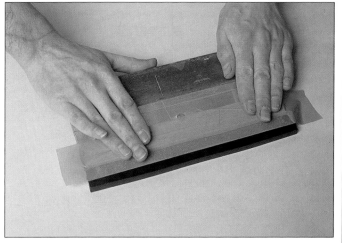

Types of blade (above)
Rubber blades need frequent sharpening; polyurethane stays sharp for longer. It is usual to fit a hand squeegee (**above**) with a soft blade. The one-arm squeegee (**top**) is likely to require a polyurethane blade. The composite squeegee (**centre**) can be fitted with different blades at the same time.

Taping the blade (top)
Taping a squeegee makes it easier to clean. It also prevents the ink from seeping into the handle groove only to reappear as streaks during subsequent printing.

Sharpening the blade (above)
The squeegee blade should be kept sharp. It can be sharpened with a home-made wood and sandpaper device or with a manufacturer's squeegee dresser. A custom-made sharpening device is illustrated above.

THE BLADE

The squeegee blade is made of either rubber, which is inexpensive but becomes blunt very quickly, or polyurethane, which maintains its sharp edge for more printings. Both types of blade come in three different grades - hard, medium and soft. Hard blades are used for printing on shiny flat surfaces that are non-absorbent, such as glass, plastic or coated board, where the minimum of spreading can be tolerated. Medium flexibility squeegees are used for printing on all absorbent surfaces, where a higher pressure is used for printing, as when using a one-arm squeegee or an automatic machine. Soft blades are ideal for hand printing since they flex to accommodate undulations in the printing stock and are sensitive to fluctuations in pressure, allowing difficult areas to be printed.

Angle of squeegee
The angle at which the squeegee is held determines the thickness of the ink deposit; the more upright the blade the thinner the deposit (**below left**), the lower the blade the thicker the ink will print (**below right**).

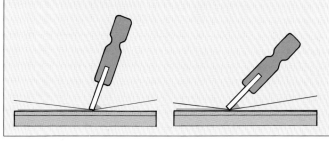

Paper for printing

Although paper is not the only stock on which limited editions or fine art prints are printed, it is the most common. Although screen inks adhere to the majority of papers and boards, it is good practice to test a new paper by printing on it and checking the ink for scuff resistance and adhesion.

As there are so many papers available, it is useful to look at the characteristics of papers in general. There are three main types of paper, hand-, mould-, and machine-made, varying widely in price and usage. A list of specialist suppliers can be found on page 140).

PAPER SURFACES

The three characteristic surfaces of paper are "hot pressed and callendered" (HP), which means that the finish is smooth, "rough", meaning textured rather like watercolour paper and "not hot press (NOT) surfaced, which has a texture between HP and rough.

The way paper has been sized, which is part of the manufacturing process, determines its degree of absorbency. The greater the absorbency of the paper, the greater the tendency of the ink to spread, possibly blurring detail. The most absorbent is "unsized" or "waterleaf". Many screenprints, however, are made on paper that is "internally sized" because it is fairly dimensionally stable and absorbs only a small quantity of ink, thereby holding detail. Internally sized papers are reasonably crease resistant and easy to clean. If necessary, absorbency can be reduced by sealing the paper with a transparent base, before applying colours.

GRAIN

The grain of the paper, determined by the direction of the fibres, also has an effect on the quality of the print. In hand-made papers the fibres adopt random directions, producing a strong, light-fast paper which provides excellent colour resolution. The disadvantages of hand-made paper are that it is very expensive, it is usually only produced in small quantities, and each sheet varies in quality so it is not suitable for large limited editions. It does have the advantage, however, that it can be pigmented in production. Mould-made paper is similar to hand-made up to the point of manufacture where rotating cylinder machines produce a product of similar quality to that made by hand, but with a quality that is constant. Unlike hand-made paper, the grain of mould-made paper has definite direction, determined by the machine on which it was made. In long-grain paper the grain runs parallel to the long edge of the paper and in short-grain paper, the grain runs parallel to the short edge.

OTHER DISTINGUISHING FEATURES

The natural deckle is the rough finished edge of the paper. On hand-made paper it is on four sides, whereas on mould-made it is only on the two outside machine edges. Natural deckles run parallel to the grain; imitation or torn deckles run at right angles to it.

Each sheet of paper has a top or "felt" side and a bottom or "wire" side. In the production process papers are often

Hand-made paper (above) David Hockney experimented in the 1970s with making his own paper. *Diving Board with Still Water on Blue Paper (1978)* is one of a series of prints on paper made by adding pigment to the paper pulp and pouring it into preformed moulds before pressing it. Thus the image became part of the paper itself.

"watermarked". Normally prints are printed on the felt side, with the watermark "right reading".

WEIGHT AND SIZE

The weight of the paper should be taken into account when making prints. If a sheet is large, it also needs to be heavy to enable it to be handled successfully. The weight of paper is expressed in grams per square metre (gsm). This is calculated by weighing 1,000 sheets of metre square paper. Thus 1,000 sheets of 400gsm paper weigh 4 kilograms. Although papers come in many weights, most limited editions are printed on sheets of 250 to 400gsm. Paper is available in heavier weights than 400gsm, but the heavier it gets, the more difficult it

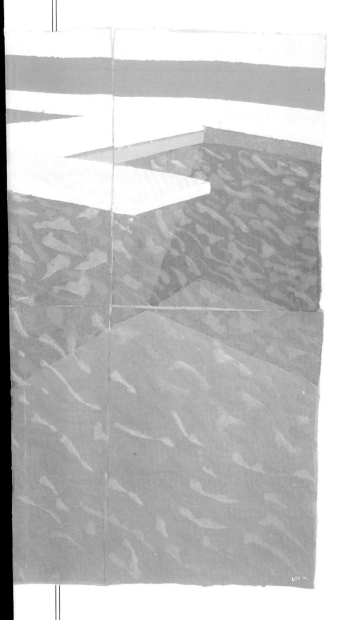

CHOOSING THE RIGHT PAPER

Machine-made papers are used for processing as well as printing. Newsprint is probably the most widely used paper in the print studio. It is used for making stencils, masking screens or vacuum beds, processing photostencils, drying wet screens, cleaning up after printing and checking print quality. Cartridge and coated papers have their everyday uses too; cartridge paper is relatively cheap, which makes it a good paper to proof on. Poster paper is thin and cheap and, as its name suggests, is mainly used for printing posters. Fine art posters however, are usually printed on matt coated paper. There are over six hundred types of coated papers and laminates in most colours — metallic, mirror foil, textured, prismatic and high gloss. These can be used to achieve special effects.

Fine art prints can be printed on any stock or surface as long as the ink is compatible, the stencil is appropriate for the image, and the mesh is of the correct count for the ink used.

Deckled paper
The edge of the paper is said to be deckled when it has a rough finish. On hand-made paper, the deckle is on four sides; mould-made paper, on two sides.

becomes to handle, which can cause problems, for example, when rolling prints for posting.

Paper comes in a number of sizes. Graphic or machine-made papers - newsprint, poster, cartridge, etc — are measured in the A series and the more expensive mould-made papers in imperial sizes ranging from 20×25in (50×62.5cm) to rolls up to 60in (150cm) wide. When deciding on print size, it is worth taking into account that most galleries have neither the means to exhibit, store nor frame very large prints.

ACIDITY

Acidity is produced by impurities or bark in wood pulp; rag papers should be acid free. The presence of acid makes the paper brittle and causes deterioration and discoloration. The acid content of paper pulp determines the pH value, which to be acid free should be above the number 7. If prints are interleaved with tissue for storage, this should also be acid free, as acid can spread through stored prints and harm them.

Inks and solvents

There are as many different inks as there are surfaces on which to print them. Every ink that is manufactured is supplied with a comprehensive data sheet covering use, so it is with the general properties of inks that this section is concerned.

OIL-BASED INKS

Most fine art prints are made using oil-based inks. These are usually matt-finished, fairly scuff-resistant, and of high pigment quality. The consistency and drying time of the ink can be controlled by the type of thinner used — fast, standard or retarder. Fast and standard thinners are used when printing at speed with, for example, a semi-automatic printing machine, requiring a correspondingly short drying time to facilitate the use of a tunnel dryer. For hand-printing, a retarding thinner allows a slower rate of printing and time to check each print without the ink drying into the mesh.

The consistency of the ink relates to the mesh count. For an average mesh (62, 77, 90), the ink should resemble engine oil; if the count is lower it should be slightly thicker, like treacle, and if it is higher than the average it should be thinned to the consistency of single cream.

FINISHES

It is possible to overprint oil-based matt colours with glossy or silk varnishes to produce different surface qualities. But silk- and medium-gloss finishes are usually obtained by using solvent-based or cellulose inks. For a really glossy effect

Inks and solvents
A glimpse of the range of hues and textures (note the gold glitter ink on the left) is seen here. Indeed there are many brands and types of inks used for different styles of printing and for a wide range of effects.

YURIKO
Cranes

This contemporary Japanese print based on traditional imagery uses modern glitter inks to express the reflective quality and movement of the splash of water. Today there is an infinite range of inks to help the artist achieve the precise effect required.

an oxidisation ink or varnish should be used, bearing in mind that they dry by chemical reaction, which requires 24 hours in the rack, and they cannot be dried in a tunnel dryer.

When mixing and overprinting with different types of inks, it is wise to test for compatibility before editioning. Sometimes an ink designed for one paper works well for another. Matt vinyl ink, designed for printing on plastics, produces a far greater matt quality when printed on paper than any other ink, so it is a good idea to experiment.

If transparent inks or varnishes are to be tinted this should be done using universal tinters, or trichromatic colours, as they are transparent. Tinters can also be used to boost colour quality as they are high-density pigments.

Metallic powders may be added to varnishes to produce silver, gold and bronze — in fact almost any mineral powder will work with these bases. To obtain a pencil line, add pow-

dered graphite to a metallic base. There are a number of special effect inks on the market; these include pearlized, expanding and glitter inks.

WATER-BASED INKS

Water-based inks, as used in schools, have an inherent disadvantage in that when printed on paper, the stock changes dimension by absorbing the water. However, concern with our environment and proposed future legislation in the United States will inevitably force ink manufacturers to develop new products that will solve these problems.

The advantages of water-based inks are that they are easily diluted with water and are much less trouble to clean up than the oil-based inks as they dissolve in water. If water-based inks are used, then care should be taken to select the appropriate stencil material (see page 40).

Planning the image

There are numerous ways of approaching the making of a screenprint. But for the inexperienced printer it may be useful to try one or two of the most common methods. The first is to rough out an idea as a drawing or as a series of preliminary sketches, and to develop this into an image that can be printed. It is important to always think in terms of the medium, in that each colour has to have an individual stencil and that unless the colour has been blended (see page 70) it is always flat, rather like gouache. The sketches should take this into account, since as soon as two or more colours are used, the question as to how to register occurs (see page 64). Generally speaking, the problems of registering colours can be minimized by conscious design decisions made at this time, for example, unsightly overlaps which may be caused by poor registration can be increased in size, and if printed with transparent colour be integrated into the print design. By using transparent inks, the tone and colour range of the print can be extended and the number of stencils reduced. Once a sketch has been made this should be turned into a full-size line drawing, from which the areas of each colour may be selected. The parameters of these colours determine the form the stencils will take and the position or size of the overprints.

The second approach is more open to chance and consequently can be more exciting and adventurous. Printing commences with a first stencil which is made intuitively and printed with a colour selected by personal taste. Subsequent stencils and the colours in which they are printed are improvized according to the critical judgement or whim of the artist, each stage suggesting further developments. This approach can be used to print both limited editions and monoprints.

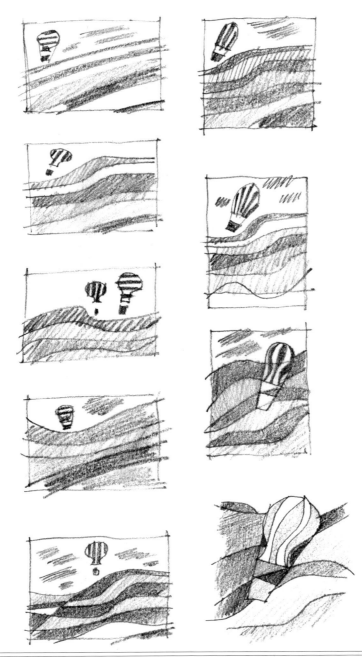

Exploring the idea
The artist Raymond Spurrier, whose print is featured on these pages said: "After the initial inspiration found while driving through the countryside in late summer, I set about trying to devise an image which could be realized using simple hand-printing equipment with registration managed entirely by eye.

I tried out various compositional options with thumbnail sketches (left). The placing of adjacent colours would demand meticulous stencil cutting and a degree of registration accuracy that seemed unlikely in the circumstances. This meant that it was necessary to make a design that took advantage of overlapping colour so the image was further abstracted into broader areas of colour."

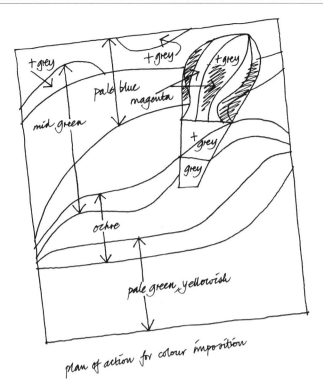

+grey

+grey

+grey

pale blue

magenta

mid green

+grey

grey

ochre

pale green, yellowish

plan of action for colour imposition

Finalizing the image
Once a suitable composition had emerged, the artist made a larger outline drawing (left) to help plan the colours and the most effective way of overlapping them. This drawing shows how he printed seven coloured stripes for the landscape using only four transparent ink colours: blue, light green, dark green and ochre. It also became clear to him that he would need only two stencils for the four colours — the blue and ochre were well separated and could therefore be cut from the same stencil with the ochre temporarily masked out while printing the blue and vice versa. The two greens were printed similarly. The balloon was printed in magenta to isolate it from the landscape, and the stripes overprinted in pale grey which is used elsewhere. The final print, *Late Summer Balloon,* is shown below.

Part Three

THE ART OF STENCIL MAKING

The stencil is the medium by which an idea, drawing, painting, photograph or existing original image may be interpreted, translated into a form which will print, and then be creatively developed.

There are three principal groups of stencils — "hand-made", which are directly applied to the screen, "autographic" and "photographic". The last two have to be processed before being attached to the screen.

Cut or torn paper stencils

Paper stencils are the simplest to make and use. They can be made from thin paper such as newsprint, detail paper or grease-proof, and they are stuck to the underside of the screen with printing ink or tape. A hole torn or cut in the centre of a sheet of newsprint attached in this way produces a positive printed image. Negative images can be produced by placing pieces of cut or torn paper on to the printing stock, lowering the screen and sticking them to the mesh using the squeegee and printing ink. More complicated designs with "floating" pieces of stencil should be stuck to the screen with filler or ink, which is allowed to dry before printing the image. Found objects such as doilies or open-weave fabrics or even cut-out strips of little men make good stencils.

One of the problems of paper stencils is that they tend to disintegrate fairly quickly. But it is possible to produce quite large editions as long as the ink is not too thin (about the consistency of engine oil) and the squeegee blade is soft. Paper stencils should not be used with coarse screens as the ink will tend to bleed, or on those that are too fine to allow the ink to penetrate sufficiently to stick the paper to the screen. Any mesh count between 42T and 90T is suitable.

Torn-paper print (**above**) The simplest form of print-making, here a square has been torn out of a piece of newsprint which has then been taped to the underside of the mesh. The figure and four symbols are floating pieces stuck to the mesh with the printing ink.

MICHAEL POTTER
Garden Room

In contrast to the simple stencil above, this sophisticated print involved photostencil work as well as overprinted colour achieved with hand-made stencils.

Stencils made with filler

S tencils have been painted on to the screen using filler since the end of the last century. It is probably the most common form of stencil-making.

Stencils made with filler usually require the artist to work negatively, ie if a brush mark is painted on to the screen, it will appear as a negative when printed. To make the process easier the design can be outlined on the mesh with a soft pencil to determine the areas which will need to be painted. Sharp edges or lines can be masked off using tape, and filler applied with a small piece of card. Fillers are usually either water soluble (for use with oil- or solvent-based inks) or spirit based (for use with water-based inks).

RED, GREEN AND BLUE FILLERS

There are three types of water-soluble filler. Red flash-dry filler as its name suggests dries instantly. Its main uses are for pre-masking and edge-filling stencils made of other mat-

Making a stencil edge with red filler
First, rule a line on the mesh with a soft pencil to show the area that needs covering. Apply filler first to the underside of the screen starting at the corner closest to you using a card sqeegee to spread the filler parallel to the frame (**top**). After two minutes to allow the filler to dry, invert the screen and treat it in the same way. Prop the frame to stop the underside sticking to the table (**above**).

erials, and for repairing or spotting leaks in stencils while the print is being printed. Green filler is a moderately fast-drying fluid, which has a high viscosity and elasticity that makes it ideal for masking, painting or retouching stencils and spotting stencils before starting to print. Blue filler is the most useful material for making hand-made stencils: it dries slowly and can be thinned extensively to enable it to be used for painting, spraying, and stippling on screens.

Water-soluble fillers can be thinned with water. A few drops of washing-up liquid can be added to help the filler flow more easily. Drying time can be reduced, if necessary, by adding 5 — 10 per cent methylated spirit to the water.

If water-based inks are to be used, filler made from a mixture of shellac flakes and methylated spirit (French polish) should be used. This filler, though more difficult to remove when dry than its water-soluble equivalent, is suitable for fine brush work and dries very quickly.

Whatever kind of filler you choose, it is important to match the thickness of filler to the mesh of the screen. The thinner the filler, the finer the mesh required; very coarse meshes may not be suitable for filler stencils as there is a risk that the resulting images will "saw tooth". In some cases it may be preferable to apply several thin coats of filler rather than a single thick coat.

Filler stencils can be applied with brushes, card squeegees, sponges or fabrics to produce textures. Spray guns (which produce negative dots) can be loaded with thinned filler and sprayed on to the screen. Contact prints may be taken from any surface which has previously been coated using a roller with the filler. Whatever method of production is used, it should be on a mesh that is capable of retaining the detail of the mark made; it would be inappropriate, for example, to spray dots on a very coarse screen. Mesh counts for filler screens range from 48T to 150T.

CELLULOSE FILLER

Another type of filler which can be exceptionally useful when changes need to be made in existing stencils, is cellulose filler. Because it is neither oil- nor water-soluble it can be used to change or re-work stencils made from other materials, which are then printed. When the image has been printed the filler can be removed using cellulose cleaner and the stencil returned to its original state.

Another use for cellulose filler is when a reverse image of the stencil is required. Use a water-solvent stencil to print the design, then apply cellulose filler to the stencil with a squeegee and allow it to dry. Finally, remove the stencil with water, leaving a new reversed stencil in its place.

FRENCH CHALK RESIST

French chalk resist stencils are a means of creating textures on existing screen images. The procedure is to sprinkle french chalk, usually through a sieve, on to the print itself. This can either be done randomly or it can be sprinkled through cut-out shapes. The screen is carefully lowered on to the chalk and ink is squeegeed across the mesh, picking up the chalk, which produces a negative image with a textured surface.

Gum and tusche method

The gum and tusche method of stencil-making has always been popular as it enables the artist to work with a positive image — ie, whatever marks are made on the screen will eventually print.

As any printer who has tried this method knows, it is very difficult to make it work satisfactorily, but this is mainly due to the fact that modern meshes have smooth threads and the proprietary fillers do not easily break down cleanly when the tusche is dissolved. Silk is better for this method than nylon or polyester as its filaments are hairy and irregular. If silk is not available, multifilament meshes work better than monofilament ones, the counts being in the range of 48T to 90T. The traditional materials for this method are tusche (a waxy black litho ink) and gum arabic. Alternatively, screenprinting ink (instead of tusche) and blue filler thinned with 5 per cent acetic acid (instead of gum arabic can be used.

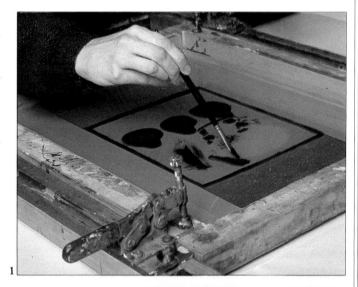

1

2

3

Gum and tusche method
This method of printing uses tusche, a black waxy litho ink, which is painted on to the top side of the screen. (1) Using whatever applicator is desired — here a brush but a sponge or rag could be used — the image is created with the tusche on the fine silk screen and left to dry. (2) Now, from the top side, traditional gum arabic is spread over the mesh and allowed to dry. (3) Using a cloth, turpentine is rubbed into both sides of the mesh, dissolving the tusche and the filler covering it. This means the areas formerly covered with tusche are now open, so that the ink can pass through.

Knife-cut stencils

The stencils are cut from sheets of adhesive film which have a removable backing sheet. This method solves the problem of "floating" pieces as the backing sheet keeps them in place until they have been adhered to the mesh. This type of stencil can be fixed to screens as coarse as 16T (for printing glitter inks) or as fine as 180T. There are four types of direct adhesion films that are suitable for making knife-cut film stencils. Of these two are iron-on, one is solvent-based and the other water-based.

Iron-on stencil films, often called stenplex stencils, are the least expensive but the most difficult to adhere to the mesh. Stenplex green is a film that can be used with all types of solvent-based inks on all kinds of fabric. Stenplex amber (or pro-film) is suitable only for oil-based inks or, if runs are very short, water-based inks. This type of film adheres best to multifilament meshes such as organdie and silk.

Solvent-based stencil films are used with oil-based or water-based inks. Water-based stencil films are used with solvent- and oil-based inks, but not water-based inks.

CUTTING THE FILM

All knife-cut films are similar in that they have a stencil layer of material laminated on to a supporting backing sheet. There are two different stencil qualities available: high tack, which can be corrected if mistakes are made, and low tack which is easier to peel but cannot be replaced if incorrectly peeled.

The image is made by cutting through the top layer and removing those areas which are to be printed. Care should be taken not to cut through the backing sheet as this may distort the stencil when it is stuck to the screen, or even prevent it sticking properly. The key to cutting this sort of stencil film is a sharp knife blade. If it is really keen, the weight of the cutting tool should be enough to cut the first layer of film and leave the backing sheet intact. Medical scalpels are particularly sharp and can be useful but care should be taken when changing blades, disposing of used ones and in the general handling of the instrument.

Once the stencil is ready, it has to be adhered to the underside of the mesh as described on the facing page. But before this can be done, the mesh should be prepared in accordance with the manufacturer's instructions (see page 26) and all traces of grease removed.

Knife-cut masking films though similar to stencil films are in fact the opposite when their function is analyzed. The masking film should be thought of as a photopositive, in which whatever remains on the backing sheet, after cutting, is what will later appear on the photostencil.

Cutting the film
Straight lines and shallow curves are more easily cut with a fixed blade knife held at a low angle (**below left**). For difficult tight curves or fine details, a swivel knife held vertically may be easier to use with practice (**below right**). If cutting angles, overcut slightly to make it easier to peel away the film.

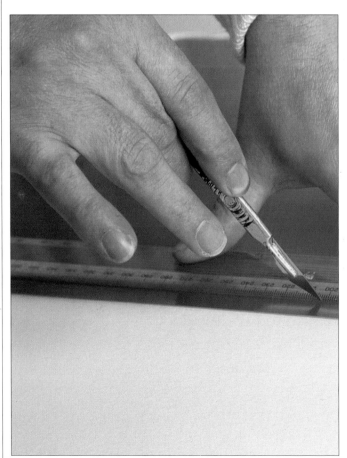

APPLYING A KNIFE-CUT STENCIL TO THE MESH

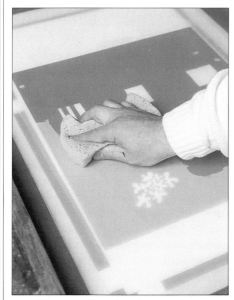 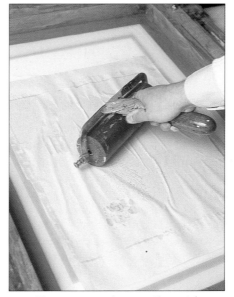 

1 The stencil is placed cut surface up on a thin raised pad, smaller than the inside dimensions of the screen, which is positioned over them. To soften the stencil material so that it sticks to the mesh — here a water-based film — water is applied with a cellulose sponge. Too much water may cause the edges of the stencil to spread.

2 To encourage the stencil to stick to the mesh, cover the top side with a sheet of paper (newsprint is ideal) and roll it with a soft rubber or gelatine roller. This will encourage the paper to absorb excess moisture and force the mesh into the body of the stencil material. Take care not to apply to much pressure with the roller or the stencil will spread and the open areas close up.

3 When the stencil is quite dry (it can be force dried using a warm air fan placed about a metre from the inside of the screen) the transparent backing sheet can be peeled off.

PATRICK CAULFIELD
Lamp and Pines

This print contains black photographic line work under which each colour was printed through a knife-cut stencil. The lamp shade was printed with ink mixed on the open screen, making each print in the edition slightly different.

Photostencils

The photostencil freed the screenprint from its early coarseness and enabled prints of great detail to be printed hundreds of times without series deterioration. Anything which can be made acceptably opaque can be used as a positive and made into a stencil that can be printed.

Before discussing photostencils in detail, it may be useful to differentiate between the terms positive, photopositive, autographic positive and photostencil.

A positive is any image, usually on a transparent or translucent base, that is opaque enough to prevent ultraviolet light from reaching photostencil material when it is placed in contact with it. Examples of materials used to make positives include black paint or photographic opaque on tracing film, red litho tape or masking film on a transparent base, amber cut stencil film, a sheet of Letraset, torn black paper, soft black crayon on tissue paper, any opaque found object and any high contrast photographs or photocopies which are on transparent film as opposed to paper. It may be slightly confusing to learn that a positive is always positive, even when the image is negative. This is because whatever constitutes the opaque element of a positive is what will eventually print.

Photopositives (as photograhic positives are known) are generated in the darkroom by enlarging existing negatives or transparencies, or by photographing original artworks on to film.

Autographic positives are drawn, painted, sprayed, collaged, frottaged or otherwise hand-made with an opaque medium on transparent or translucent material.

Photostencils are the means by which all of these types of positive can be made into printable images. This is done by placing the positive in direct contact (preferably in a vacuum frame with photostencil material and exposing both to ultraviolet light through the back of the positive. The resultant stencil is then applied to the screen. As for other types of stencil, the screen has to be selected for mesh count and prepared before a photostencil can be applied to it. The photostencil has to be dried, masked, and spotted before being printed.

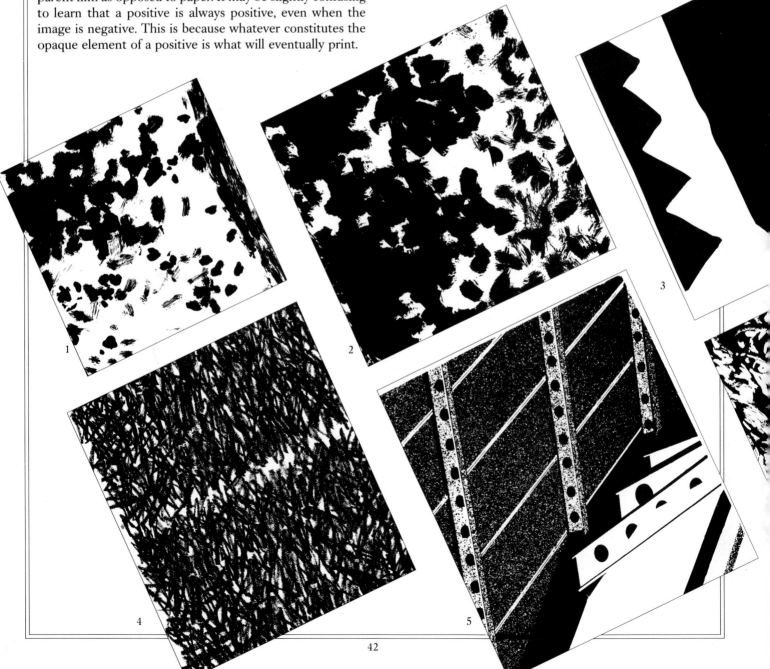

1

2

3

4

5

Positives

These positives were made in a number of ways. Opaque black ink was painted on to transparent film with a small brush (1) and a larger brush (2). A photostrip positive was used which allowed the artist to strip off certain areas and handspray them (3). A soft crayon was used on textured film (4). Hand-sprayed red masking film (5). This photostrip positive was progressively stripped off for further working (6). A photographically produced half-tone positive (7).

6

7

Methods and materials for photostencils

There are four types of photostencil material for making screenprint stencils: direct, indirect, capillary, and direct/indirect.

DIRECT PHOTOSTENCILS

Direct stencils are the least expensive of the photostencils and are relatively easy to process. They must be used if water-based or textile inks are required. Direct stencils are made with ultraviolet-light-sensitive emulsion which is applied to the whole screen and allowed to dry under light-safe conditions. A positive is then placed in contact with the underside of the screen and held tightly against the emulsion by a copy sac, a grapho screen or a printer frame and is exposed to ultraviolet light.

The positive should always be correctly placed in relation to the emulsion on the screen. A photopositive is usually placed emulsion to emulsion. Painted or drawn stencils have the worked surface against the emulsion. The emulsion is chemically altered only where the light passes through the positive. It remains water soluble where it has been masked by the opaque parts of the positive. The still soluble emulsion is then removed by rinsing with hot water and leaves a stencil that, when dried, masked and spotted, can be printed.

If professional equipment is unavailable, small-scale direct stencils can be made in the same way by applying the emulsion but then using a sheet of 10mm float glass and a flexible pad, over which the frame fits, to support the mesh and positive. The weight of the glass holds the positive in position. The light source could either be a photoflood (see facing page), an ultraviolet lamp, or even the sun. Exposure times are a matter for experiment but the midday sun should take about 10 minutes.

INDIRECT PHOTOSTENCILS

Indirect photostencil film comes in the form of a roll of light-sensitive film, supported on a transparent backing sheet. The

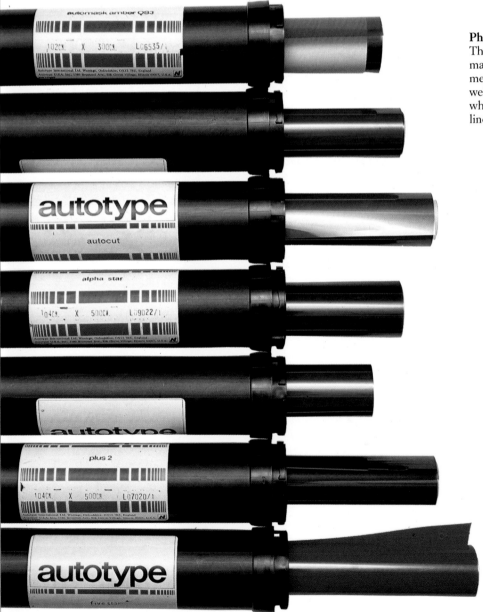

Photostencil materials
There is a wide range of photostencil materials suited to all types of printing methods. Some are designed to adhere well or to stand up to long print runs, while others are particularly suited to fine line or half-tone work.

process for making an indirect photostencil is similar to that for a direct photostencil except that it is made away from the screen and attached to it after it has been developed. For indirect photostencils the positive is positioned so that the emulsion side is touching the backing side of the film. The positive and film are placed in the printer frame so that the light from the exposure source passes through the back of the positive and through the back of the stencil film to activate the emulsion. The opaque areas of the positive prevent light from activating the emulsion of the stencil film. Those areas exposed to light do not wash out when the film is processed.

The method of processing depends on film type. Some films need to be developed for one minute in hydrogen peroxide (20 vol) which further hardens those areas exposed to the light. Then the film is rinsed with hot water until the areas of emulsion that were covered by the positive have been thoroughly removed. The film is given a final rinse with cold water to remove any residual stencil material and to return the stencil to its pre-heated size. It is important to ensure that all the unexposed emulsion is washed away before the stencil is applied to the screen because, if this is inadequately done, the residue will dry into the mesh and form a scum in the fabric that will prevent the ink from passing through the open mesh.

CAPILLARY FILM

This is also used for the indirect method and comes on a roll. A piece larger than the positive is cut and placed on a raised pad emulsion side up. The screen, ink side up, is placed over it and the film is made wet from the inside of the screen with a sponge, which draws the stencil on to the mesh. Any excess water is squeegeed off and the screen is dried under light-safe conditions (amber).

The capillary stencil provides accurate registration and it is very sensitive to detail. It also has the advantage over all indirect films in that it can be cut to the required size. Extra thick deposits of ink can be achieved with the capillary stencil by applying an emulsion coat to the printing side of the screen after the sheet film has dried. Once dry, capillary film is exposed and processed like a direct film.

DIRECT/INDIRECT PHOTOSTENCIL

The direct/indirect stencil film is bonded to the mesh with photostencil emulsion, which is applied with a soft, rounded squeegee to the ink side of the screen. The method of application — using a raised pad, light-safe drying and the subsequent exposure — is the same as for the capillary film.

WHICH FILM TO USE

All photostencil films have advantages and disadvantages so it is important to experiment to find out which is the most suitable for any individual printmaker. The indirect film is the most consistent in quality and has the ability to produce fine detail. It has the added advantage that it is ready for exposure and does not require elaborate equipment, as only the stencil is exposed and washed out, rather than the screen. Indirect stencils are also easier to remove from the screen when printing has been completed.

Light Source

The type of light source used to expose the stencil film will affect the eventual quality of the stencil. A point source from one lamp will produce a better result than a number of sources. For example, Actinic blue tubes in textile exposure frames produce an inferior stencil to a halide lamp.

The best source is the metal halide lamp which is available in 2 and 5 Kilowatt models. (The latter can be switched to 2 Kilowatt for use with materials such as daylight film.) However a fairly efficient home-made light source can be made using a photoflood. But make sure it is correctly wired using the manufacturer's recommended components.

Place the light source above the vacuum frame at a distance equal to the diagonal of the largest stencil.

Care should be taken to replace the bulbs in any light source as deterioration leads to pinholes in stencil materials.

Using either a pre-processed screen or a piece of photostencil film, exposures can be made using sunlight as a light source. Invert the screen on a raised pad, placing the positive on the screen, covered with a sheet of glass to hold the positive in contact with the screen. Exposure time can be as long as an hour but you will need to experiment.

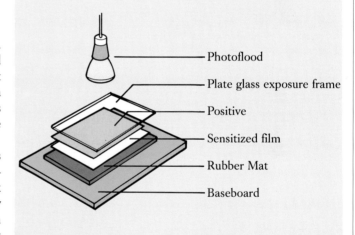

- Photoflood
- Plate glass exposure frame
- Positive
- Sensitized film
- Rubber Mat
- Baseboard

MAKING AN INDIRECT PHOTOSTENCIL

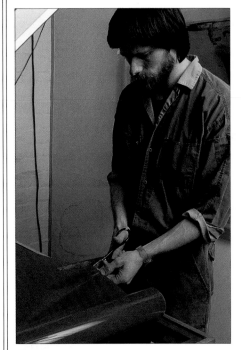

1 To make an indirect photostencil, the roll of light-sensitive film, supported on a transparent backing sheet, is cut to the right size, allowing at least 5cm extra around the positive.

2 Now the film is placed in the printing frame on top of the positive with the backing side down on the emulsion side of the positive.

3 Here the printing frame is being released into the vertical position prior to exposure. The vacuum has now been switched on to hold the two films hard against each other to prevent the light scattering.

5 The film is rinsed with hot water until the areas of emulsion that were covered by the opaque positive and therefore not affected by the light have been thoroughly removed. A final rinse with cold water returns the film to its original size and washes out any residual stencil material.

6 Having checked that all particles of the unexposed emulsion have been rinsed from the stencil, it is carefully positioned on the under side of the screen.

4 After exposure, some films at this stage need to be processed for one minute in a bath of hydrogen peroxide (20 vol). This further hardens those areas of the film exposed to the light.

7 The stencil is fixed to the screen by laying a sheet of newsprint over it and rolling it gently but firmly with a roller to squeeze out the moisture and force the softened stencil into the mesh.

8 Drying can be assisted by a fan heater from the printing side. Once dry, the transparent backing sheet can be removed from the stencil film.

Autographic positives

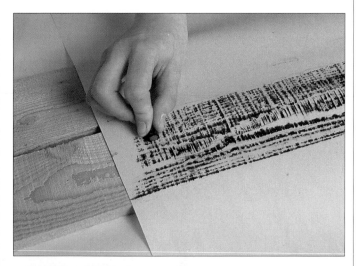

Autographic positives are hand-made by the artist with opaque materials on transparent or translucent backings. It is the modern equivalent of the serigraph. The marks made by the artist are accurately translated by the stencil to create a printed image which is a true reflection of the artist's work.

The autographic stencil can be made in any number of ways such as painting with opaque ink on to tracing film (see Chapter 5), by spraying with an airbrush or spray gun on to film, by drawing directly on to film with soft black crayons (toothed tracing film is available which is rather like drawing on a litho plate), by taking rubbings with black waxy crayons to produce textures (frottage), by collaging discrete forms to produce an amalgamated image, stippling with a sponge or fabric or simply coating objects with black ink and contact printing them on to tracing film. Pre-worked screen stencils can be printed on to transparent sheets, with any colour that is UV safe — black, red, amber — and re-worked to produce new stencils. The possibilities are endless.

Frottage (right)
The artist intends to include a textured area like knotted wood as part of an autographic stencil. A sheet of thin tracing film (002) is placed over a piece of pine

and the texture is picked up by rubbing it over with a soft black waxy crayon (**above right**). This frottage may then be used as an autographic positive with a photostencil (**right**).

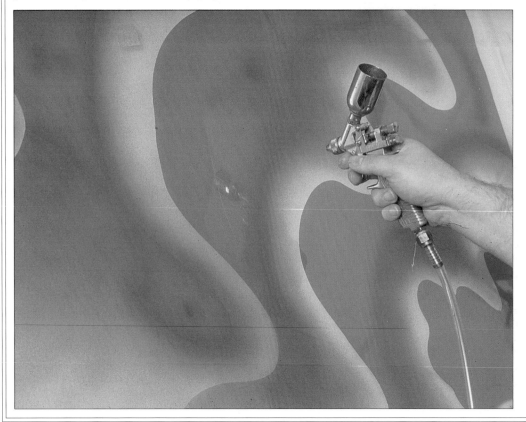

Spraying (left)
Spraying is used in the stencil-making process to approximate continuous tone. Use a medium that is opaque to ultraviolet light. Black ink is completely opaque but red or orange masking fluid (used here) is slightly translucent so the artist can see what is beneath.

TERRY WILSON
Anonymous Portraits 5 and 6

Autographic screenprints made by
drawing and painting onto the stencils.
The paint was applied using a range of
techniques — flicked with a paintbrush
and splattered with a toothbrush.

Photopositives

The potential range of photopositive is so vast, that to effect even an introduction to it requires a minimal photographic knowledge. Before attempting to make photostencils, the artist should understand about the timing of exposure, aperture opening, depth of field, grain size relative to film spread and have a rudimentary knowledge of developing and printing photographs. The most basic photopositive can be made by placing opaque objects on a sheet of high-contrast lith film (see below), which is then exposed, developed and fixed. But the simplest truly photographic image can be made by enlarging 35mm black and white negative film on to lith film. Incidentally, if a high-contrast photographic print or photocopier print is coated with liquid paraffin on the back, the paper becomes transparent enough to use as a positive. This does not work with resin-coated papers.

PHOTOGRAPHIC IMAGES

Film positives provide the opportunity to combine photographic and autographic images. There are two types of photographic image, continuous tone and line. A continuous tone film is familiar to anyone with a camera — it is the "normal" type of film which reproduces all tones from black to white. Line film, on the other hand, reduces the image to black and white, like a silhouette. The implication of continuous tone is that every possible tone from black to white (or colour) is on the negative. If the negative is magnified, however, it will be found to be made up of tiny, similarly toned particles, which are more concentrated in the dark areas than the light.

CAMERAS AND ENLARGERS

To make a photopositive first the image is photographed with a camera. The image may be some artwork or a painting or simply a person or landscape. This image is developed on to continuous tone or line film which is then enlarged on to photostencil film.

There are many different makes of camera and enlarger which will produce reasonable positives. The range of 35mm, 2¼in square, 5×4in and 10×8in formats are all usable with any of the films mentioned in this section. The only thing to bear in mind when purchasing equipment for enlarging, other than cost, is that the larger the format of the negative, the higher the quality of the positive and the more flexible the system for experimentation — it is difficult to mask or register 35mm film, but relatively easy to do it with a 10×8in film. A positive register system, made by punching a set of holes which correspond to pins in the head of the enlarger, enables a number of films to be exposed in absolute registration. It is worth remembering too that an enlarger can double up as a camera if it is fitted with copy lights.

HALF-TONE

In printing, inks cannot reproduce continuous tone so it has to be approximated by breaking the tonal range of the image into distinct dots or marks which are quantified — 90 per cent dots = dark, 10 per cent dots = light. The most common use of this method — known as half-tone printing — is seen every day in newspaper photographs and advertising posters.

The half-tone effect is achieved by placing a half screen in contact with either the negative in the carrier or the image on

ALLEN JONES
Car '68

The point of departure for this 1960s car was a photograph developed on continuous tone film which was then enlarged on to photostencil film with a half-tone screen interposed to make the positive.

BEN JOHNSON
Sainsbury Centre

Here the perforations in the blinds impose
their own grids of dots vying with the
much smaller dots of the half-tone screen.
To maintain the colour subtlety of the
original photographic image, this four-
colour separation was printed with tinted
colours rather than the trichromatic
colours and then three intermediate
separations were added.

the bed of the enlarger, or by interposing a screen between the artwork and the film in the camera back if a process camera is used. This contact screen breaks up the image into a regular dot matrix in the case of a half screen and an irregular dot in the case of mezzotint. The regular dot pattern of the half-screen is very difficult to work by hand. Consequently the artist may find the mezzotint, with its affinity to sprayed dots, more useful if creative decisions are to be made and effected.

Dot matrix stencils always produce moiré patterns if one of them is overprinted with another. To limit this the mezzotint screen should be moved through at least 10 per cent each time a new positive is made from the same source material. In the case of the four-colour half-tone reprographic process, the screens are moved through 30°, 15°, 15°, as the rulings on the screen for the yellow printer are angled at 45°, the magenta 75°, the black 90° and the blue 105° to any common side. If half-tone positives are applied to the mesh, they should be rotated until coinciding moiré with the mesh fabric is eliminated; this may mean that an image will have to be placed diagonally on the screen.

POSTERIZATION

Posterization is an alternative way of creating an illusion of continuous tone. This is achieved by printing a number of over- and under-exposed line film positives made from the same negative with sequential exposure. To exploit this a continuous tone negative or transparency is projected on to a sheet of light-sensitive film and a test strip is made using a number of exposure times. A selection of these exposure times is made with the intention of producing evenly spaced, tonal separation. These separations are then enlarged to produce positives — the greater the number, the closer the approximation to continuous tone. If enlargements are made using positive material (eg colour transparencies) it is advisable to work with full-size negatives as they are easier to hand work, and at any time new positives can be made by merely contact printing them; it is exceedingly difficult to re-size an enlargement once the image has been removed from the carrier. When posterizations are printed, opaque inks can be used to print from light to dark, or transparent inks can be similarly used or printed in reverse order from dark to light.

GERD WINNER
Harrison's Wharf

The technique used here is more
sophisticated than conventional
posterization in that negative masks were
used to eliminate some areas of colour.

WENDY TAYLOR
Iguana

Posterizations made from a pastel drawing
were printed with transparent inks from
dark to light to create a continuous tone effect.

ANDREW HOLMES
Thermo King

A combination of posterized,
photographic and hand-cut stencils on to
which the artist has added further hand-
made painted stencils were used for this image.

Stencil films for photopositives

For the purpose of making photopositives, you need black on transparent film base, which is in fact pink due to an anti-halation backing that remains until they are fixed. There are, of course, many types of film available that are not mentioned here. The films discussed below are best for the artist or small studio as they can all be processed using the same chemicals.

LITH FILM

Orthochromatic film is a high contrast film that can be processed under red-safe lighting conditions in a processor or by hand using conventional dish developer, stop and fixative. Lith film produces an image that is either black or transparent; there are no intermediate tones. When exposed to continuous tone negatives and transparencies, the ratio of developed black film to transparent base can be adjusted by altering exposure and development times.

There are two basic types of lith film — general purpose orthochromatic and panchromatic. General purpose orthochromatic lith film is the most useful for hand processing as it permits a wide latitude in exposure and development. Panchromatic film is principally used with filters to produce colour-separated stencils for four-colour printing (see below right). Because of its sensitivity to the whole colour spectrum, panchromatic film needs to be processed in total darkness. Although it is sometimes recommended for use with a dark green filter, this is of little practical use. Both are available with thick and thin backing sheets or bases. If work is to be tightly registered, the thick base film, which is more expensive, is slightly more stable. The thin base films can be used to reverse images by exposing through the back. Both types of film can be processed by hand, but also come in rapid access form that is used for automatic film processing.

DUPLICATING FILM

Another type of film used for creating photostencils is duplicating film. This is also orthochromatic (ie, it may be used with red light). It is a reversal film which produces a positive image from a positive original or a negative from a negative original. So if a colour transparency is placed in an enlarger and projected on to duplicating film, it will be reproduced as a black and tonal transparency. As this is a reversal film, underexposure produces an image that is too dark, and over-exposure one that is too light.

DAYLIGHT FILM

A most useful contact film, if a UV light source and contact frame is available, is a daylight film — positive or negative. Positive film produces the same image to that which is contact printed, a particular use being to increase the contrast of drawings which are too light; negative film produces the opposite image.

AUTO-SCREEN FILM

If half-tone positives are needed, and screens to produce them are unavailable, there is a film called "auto-screen", a negative film with a dot matrix applied.

STENCILS FOR FOUR-COLOUR SEPARATION

This is the system that is used to print most colour artwork and photography in books, magazines and posters. In simple terms, it is based on the principle of photographing the original colour image through a series of filters — red, blue and green — that produce positives that print respectively only cyan, yellow and magenta (the three printing colours). The fourth colour is black, which is produced by exposing all three filters in sequence on to the same negative.

The colour filters required for four-colour separation are red filters numbers 23A, 24 and 29, blue filters numbers 47 and 47B, and green filters numbers 58 and 61. Colour separation requires particularly conscientious film processing as the slightest variation in exposure times can produce a colour bias in the positive that when printed may lead to a muddy image. This is caused by degraded colour in both the photographic and printing stages.

When making your own four-colour separations, it is a good idea to develop a simple system that enables you to identify each filtered negative and its respective positive. For example, if no corners are cut off the red filter negative and its corresponding cyan positive, you may then cut one corner from the blue filter negative and the yellow positive, two corners from the green negative and the magenta positive, and three corners from the black negative and positive.

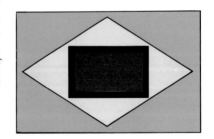

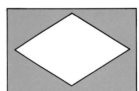

Red filter

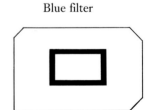

Blue filter

Green filter

All filters

Colour separation
The original colour image (1) is photographed through a red filter to produce a cyan positive (2), a blue filter for the yellow positive (3) a green filter for a magenta positive (4) and, finally the black positive is produced by exposing all three filters in sequence on to the same negative (5). To identify each filtered negative and its respective positive, cut off the corners progressively.

Developing photostencils

As has already been mentioned, the films discussed can all be processed with the same chemicals which are suitable for the artist or small studio. Lith developer usually comes in two packs, A and B, each of which is diluted 3 parts water to 1 part chemical, before being mixed together to produce the working solution. (Rapid access developers are usually sold in a single pack ready for use.) Developers have a recommended working temperature of 20°C. However, if they are slightly warmer, 21-22°C, a greater range of exposed images may be produced from the same source material such as a negative.

Photographic work should be completed in small batches because developers start to oxidize and deteriorate as soon as they are mixed. The optimum development range for lith materials is between 2½ and 3 minutes. It is best to consult the manufacturer's information sheet provided with each film. The state of the developer can be observed in the time it takes for the image to appear on the film. Normally, this should be

Developing the film
The photopositive film is developed in a shallow dish containing lith developer diluted with water as recommended (**below left**). The image should appear after 45 to 60 seconds (**below right**).

between 45 and 60 seconds into the development time. If it takes longer, the developer needs renewing.

If a contrasting image is required, the developer should be vigorously agitated in the dish, taking care not to splash it. Detail can be achieved with the "fine line technique" which involves the gentle agitation of the dish until the image appears and intermittent agitation (5 seconds in every 30) until the image is fully developed.

A stop bath negates the action of the developer and thereby prolongs the life of the fixative. Stop has a colour indicator which changes when it needs renewing. It can be stored after use until that time.

FIXATIVE

Fixative should be diluted in the ratio of 3 parts water to 1 part fixative. A rule of thumb is that film should be in the solution three times the clearing time of the anti-halation backing so, if it takes 20 seconds for the pink backing to go transparent, the film should be left another 40 seconds. Fixative can be stored after use until it begins to take too long to clear. The fixed positive should be washed for about 10 minutes in running water and dried, preferably in a dust-free cabinet.

The processing of positives in the darkroom and the manipulation of the images produced is an area open to creativity and experimentation. In the darkroom, the ability to actually see what is happening in the developer can be improved by under-lighting the development dish with a safe light.

Darkroom layout should be practical in as much as one process should lead to another. A surface on which film can be placed or cut should be adjacent to the enlarger. The development sequence of develop, stop, fix and wash should be arranged so that the operator knows where everything is even in total darkness.

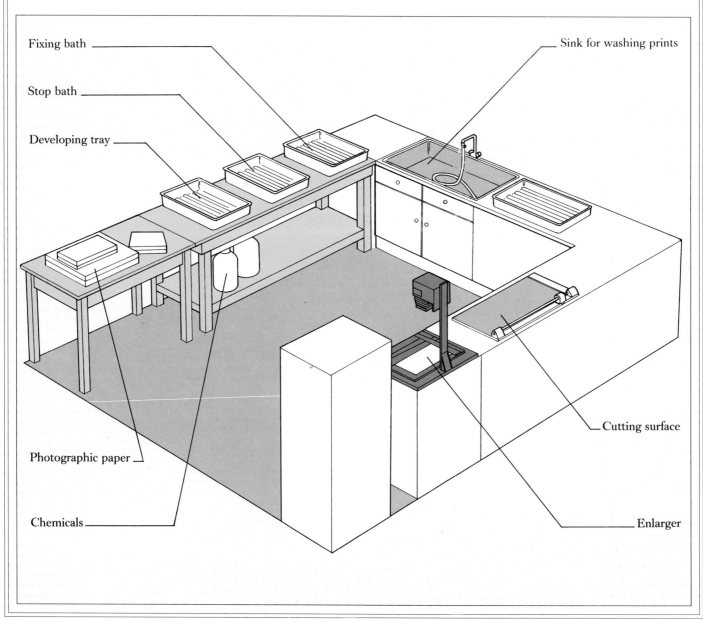

Fixing bath

Stop bath

Developing tray

Photographic paper

Chemicals

Sink for washing prints

Cutting surface

Enlarger

TIPS ABOUT STENCILS

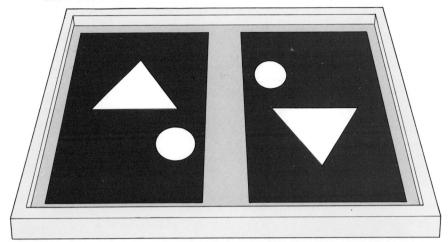

■ As a general rule the quality of the stencil will determine the mesh count of the screen: a fine half-tone image cannot be applied to a coarse screen. Usually the relationship of image to mesh is one which can be determined by common sense.

■ Whatever type of stencil is used, care should be taken positioning it on the screen. A stencil should never be placed too close to the frame and an adequate ink reservoir must always be available at both ends of the squeegee run. A general working guide is that there should be at least 10cm on either side of the running edges, and a reservoir of about quarter the length of the open area at each end of the print stroke.

■ If two or more large images are placed on single screens they should be oriented to provide ease of masking while each is being printed. They should also be placed mirror fashion in the same position relative to the edges of the frame, so that the printer only needs to turn the frame through 180° and the second image is in approximate register. The position of large images on the screen should be carefully predetermined, as it is unfortunate to find that an image has been placed in such a way that it hangs off the end of the table and cannot be registered.

■ If a number of colours are to be printed with the same screen, they should be in register with one another so that the printer will only need to register the image once; any other colours on the same screen will only need slight adjustments to correct their registration.

■ If two or more small areas of different colours are on the same stencil, it is a good idea to try and print them together, as this will reduce the number of times the print has to be handled and registered.

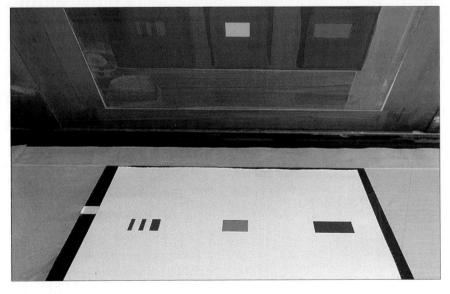

Part Four

PRINTING THE IMAGE

To print successfully you first need the right equipment. This need not be expensive; many items can be made at home. Equally important is arranging a convenient studio layout and maintaining an orderly approach to your printmaking.

The printing table

There are as many different designs for home-made tables as there are for home print studios. The advantages of the system illustrated here is that screens of different sizes can be easily fitted with the G-clamp on to the hingebar. Provision for "lift off" (the gap between the screen and print bed) is determined by the height at which the rear of the frame is clamped. The front lift may be provided by cardboard stuck with double-sided tape to the front corners of the screen. The counterbalance system means that the front of the bed is not encumbered with stays.

The points to consider with regard to any printing table are that the rear hinge assembly should be strong enough not to move so that front to back registration can be maintained. It should also have a master frame on to which different sizes of screen can be rigidly clamped. Finally, lateral movement should be prevented by a positive front locking system. The table itself should be solid enough to prevent movement or "flexing" while printing and have a quiet vacuum motor attached to a vacuum base, to hold the paper and effect lift off.

If a commercially produced table is bought, it should, however, be as large as is practical, not only to make large images but also to allow small prints to be printed in different positions. Large frames enable a number of stencils to be used with only one screen, the print being registered in different positions underneath it. The counterbalance system should be adjustable to allow the operator to lift the screen with a minimum of effort.

The vacuum base, a thin rectangular box with holes on the top side attached to a vacuum pump below, provides suction to hold the paper still while printing, and to prevent the paper sticking to the screen once it has been printed with ink. The vacuum and lift off together determine the quality of ink deposit and, on commercially produced machines, the vacuum is operated automatically only when the image is printed and when the screen is raised the vacuum automatically shuts off so that the paper can be easily registered. The master frame should be adjustable in height, to enable different thicknesses of stock to be printed underneath it and most importantly to allow for lift off. The vacuum motor should be quiet in operation, and be powerful enough to hold the largest sheet of paper, printed all over with thick ink.

LIFT OFF

"Lift off", "off contact", or "snap" are different names for the gap between the underside of the screen and the print bed. The reason for having this gap is that, without it, ink would flood under or bleed into the image when a print was pulled. As the squeegee is pulled across the screen, the front edge of its printing blade forces the mesh into contact with the stock, forcing the ink through the mesh and the stencil. As the squeegee passes across the mesh, the fabric behind the blade lifts off the printed image.

The height of the lift off is determined by a number of factors, such as the size of screen, the extent of the open area of the stencil, the tension of the mesh, the thickness of the ink and the pull of the vacuum. The screen size and open printing area of a large screen will require more lift off than a small one. The tighter the fabric is stretched over the frame, the smaller the gap needs to be. Thick ink tends to behave like glue, sticking the paper to the screen unless the vacuum is efficient. Thin ink on the other hand lifts off easily. The vacuum will not work efficiently if the holes around the edge of the stock are not properly masked out.

The height of the lift off also affects the accuracy of the registration, as the greater the gap, the more the stencil distorts. The lift off should never be so high that the printer has to force the mesh down on to the bed. If so, the stencil may be fractured by the edge of the squeegee blade.

If an artist wishes to print on a vertical surface such as a stretched canvas or a piece of sculpture, lift off can be achieved by sticking pieces of card to the underside corners of the frame with double-sided tape. The thickness of the card should be determined by the size of the stencil; a rough guide is 3mm of thickness of card to 2.5cm of stencil.

Home-made printing table
A conventional printing surface can be made with a sheet of 2cm thick Formica-laminated chipboard, 15cm larger all round than the maximum size of paper you intend to print. Fix this to any sturdy table. A hingebar made with a 5 × 5cm section block of wood should be attached by large hinges to one end of the board. Clamp the screen to this with two G-clamps fixing a weight with wire to the threaded handle of the clamp to counterbalance the screen. A home-made vacuum bed can be made with a domestic vacuum cleaner.

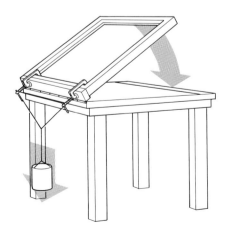

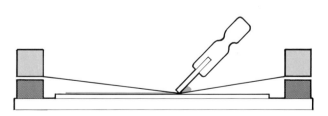

Lift off
It is essential that there is a gap between the screen and print bed to prevent the ink flooding under the stencil. This gap is known as lift off.

Getting ready for printing

During the course of printing the following materials should be handy: masking tape, sticking tape, invisible tape and double-sided tape. Masking tape is used in any circumstances when a low tack is required as it is easily removed. It should not have direct contact with the ink. Sticking tape and invisible tape are used on or under the printing surface to mask or correct stencils. (Note that tape can be used on the underside of the screen with indirect stencils to remove parts of them deliberately.) Blue and red filler plus brushes should be available to make any corrections or to spot any leaks during printing. A ruler, pencil, scissors and knife are usually needed during the initial registering of the stencil.

To facilitate printing, a squeegee no larger than 5cm either side of the image should be used, as the longer it is, the more effort is needed to manipulate it in printing. A number of palette knives will be needed, their size will depend on the volume of ink mixed (1 litre tins use 15cm blades and 5 litre 25cm), as will ink containers. If solvent- or oil-based inks are

used, containers should be made of tin or polypropylene, not plastic. The rag for cleaning up should be absorbent cotton. Many of the new paper substitutes are not absorbent enough, and merely move the ink about on the screen. Finally, a large pile of newsprint should be available to test the quality of the printed image, rectify any mistakes such as "tears" from the back of the squeegee (these may be blotted and then reprinted) and for cleaning up.

DRYING RACKS

The paper on which an edition is to be printed and the rack in which it is to be stored while drying should be as close to the print table as possible to minimize effort by the printer.

There are three different types of rack: the ball rack (or its equivalent which may be home-made with wires and pegs); the studio drying rack, which is a series of spring-loaded trays; and the tunnel dryer, a conveyor belt which takes wet prints through heater and cooler units and stacks them dry at the end of the belt.

Tunnel dryer
This method of drying prints is generally found where printing is executed on a large scale. The wet prints are placed singly on a conveyor belt which carries them through heater and cooler units to stack them dry at the end.

Studio drying rack
Left This drying system consists of a series of spring loaded trays on to which single prints are laid to dry. The detail shows how the prints should be allowed to project by 7 cm from the front of the trays to make de-racking easier.

STUDIO LAYOUT

The studio should be set out in such a way that the need to move around it is minimized. As each individual studio will have its requirements determined by its area and the amount and type of equipment used, to do more than show a schematic layout is impractical. This layout shows what is necessary, and what to avoid. Most of its recommendations are a matter of common sense — wet processing should not be adjacent to paper storage, ink mixing should be carried out in daylight conditions or at least in a constant colour-corrected artificially-lit area. Some processes have health and safety implications such as ultraviolet light sources, from which operators must be screened. Darkrooms and any wet areas in which electricity and water are used together must be protected by a micro-circuit breaker (MCB).

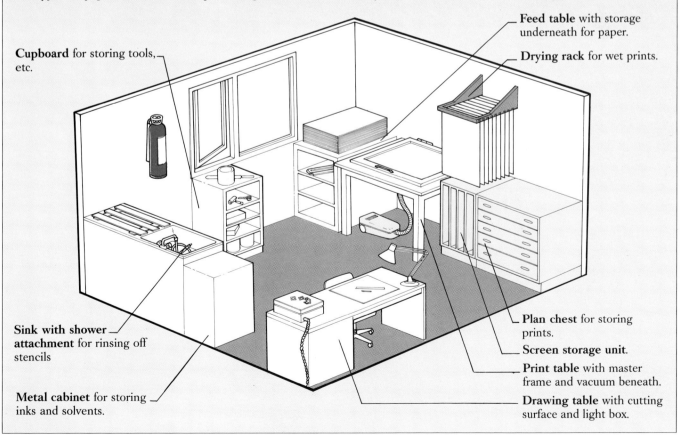

Cupboard for storing tools, etc.

Sink with shower attachment for rinsing off stencils

Metal cabinet for storing inks and solvents.

Feed table with storage underneath for paper.

Drying rack for wet prints.

Plan chest for storing prints.

Screen storage unit.

Print table with master frame and vacuum beneath.

Drawing table with cutting surface and light box.

Taking a print

The print bed should generally be set up so that the stock, the printing surface and the mesh are parallel. If one edge of the screen is higher than the other, the resulting image will be "out of true" or distorted.

If professionally made tables are used, you may find it easier to print if the back of the table is raised by about 30cm using bricks. This has the effect of reducing the stretch for the printer to the back of the screen, aiding the pull pressure by encouraging the printer to use his weight, as well as strength, to pull the print down hill. This makes long print runs a lot less tiring to produce. In addition, visual registration is made easier as it reduces parallax (see page 64). Also, if a one-arm squeegee is used, the tendency for the ink to run to the back of the screen is reduced. Finally, it has the unexpected bonus of preventing the print table from becoming a surface on which things are stored.

Although there are other ways of printing, the method outlined on this page is generally regarded as the cleanest and most efficient. The screen is always kept wet, so there is no "drying in" problem, and the ink is printed for only a minimum distance; it is tiring and fruitless to pull ink across large tracts of screen where there is no stencil image. Furthermore, the ink should not reach the front or back of the frame so that the squeegee handle and the printer's hands remain ink-free.

Larger images are more easily printed laterally using a one-arm squeegee attached to the back of the table on an arm. If this type of squeegee is used, the system of flooding and printing is similar to that of hand printing but the print stroke should travel towards the register corner of the stock. This is known as printing into "lay".

Taking a hand pull
With everything ready to print, the ink is poured with the aid of a palette knife into the reservoir (1). To charge the screen with ink prior to printing, lift the front of the screen and with the other hand place the squeegee behind the ink and, keeping it at a low angle and with minimal pressure, push it away from you across the stencil and beyond it about 5cm (2). At the end of this "flood" coat, lift the squeegee cleanly to break the surface tension of the ink (3). Having lowered the screen, using both hands with a firm even pressure pull the squeegee towards you to take your print (4). Once again lift the squeegee cleanly off the mesh to prevent the ink from dripping (5).